# Know Your Horses

**Rand McNally & Company**
Chicago · New York · San Francisco

# Family of the Horse

The geological history of the earth — during which time the present-day oceans and land masses evolved — covers many millions of years. Geologists and prehistorians have divided this whole period into a number of eras or epochs that are universally named. The most recent of these is the Quaternary which began about two million years ago. Immediately before that was the Tertiary period which began about seventy million years ago.

The Tertiary period was a time of tremendous change. The two poles were growing cooler while the lands on the equator remained warm. The continents, which had been slowly drifting across the seas in earlier eras, now began to settle into the positions they occupy today. On land, mountains started to emerge and volcanoes appeared. Luxurious vegetation began to abound.

This was not a period of brutal conflict between aggressive animals. The ferocious battles of the dinosaurs were already part of the past, and their place had been taken by tiny, furry animals which suckled their young and automatically controlled their body temperatures. These were the first mammals.

About ten million years after the decline of the dinosaurs, mammals had become the rulers of the world. Several separate species had developed, including fierce carnivores (flesheaters) and a variety of early mammalian herbivores (planteaters). Among these were the primitive types like the rhinoceros, the elephant, and the horse.

The horse's ancestor, Eohippus (known as "the dawn horse,"), first appeared in the primeval forests of Europe and North America some sixty million years ago.

In many ways, Eohippus (scientists also call it Hyracotherium) so little resembled the modern horse that we should find it almost impossible to recognize it as the ancestor of the graceful animal we know today. It was an easily frightened animal no larger than a fox. It had four toes on its front feet and three on its hind, and it lived in the forests, browsing on lush ferns and leafy boughs which grew in such profusion.

Scientists believe that Eohippus was striped so that it could blend in with the shadows of the trees. This was probably its main method of defense for it did not have great speed to avoid predators. Eohippus did have one other advantage. The broad, fleshy pads on its feet enabled it to move silently through the forest.

In the millions of years that followed, more advanced types of horse evolved. These

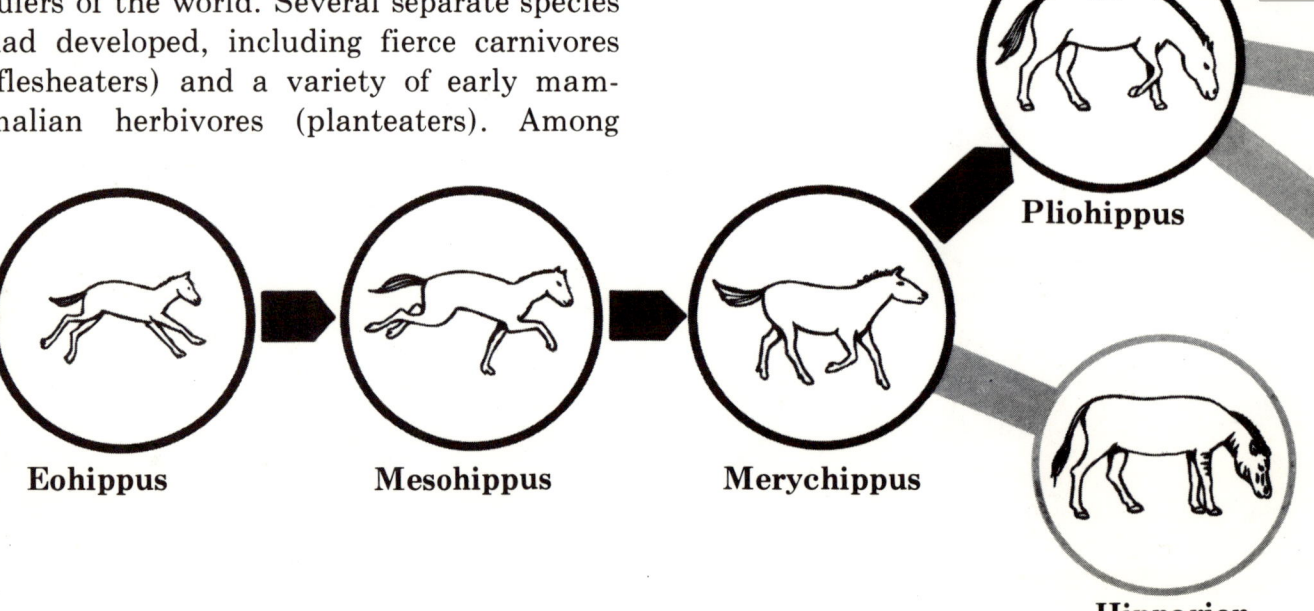

Eohippus → Mesohippus → Merychippus → Pliohippus

Hipparion

lived on the plains as opposed to the forests. Their teeth changed as their eating habits altered, for now horses were consuming grass instead of leaves. They also began to lose the toes on their feet and to develop hooves instead. One such descendant of Eohippus became the ancestor of the true horse. Its name was Pliohippus.

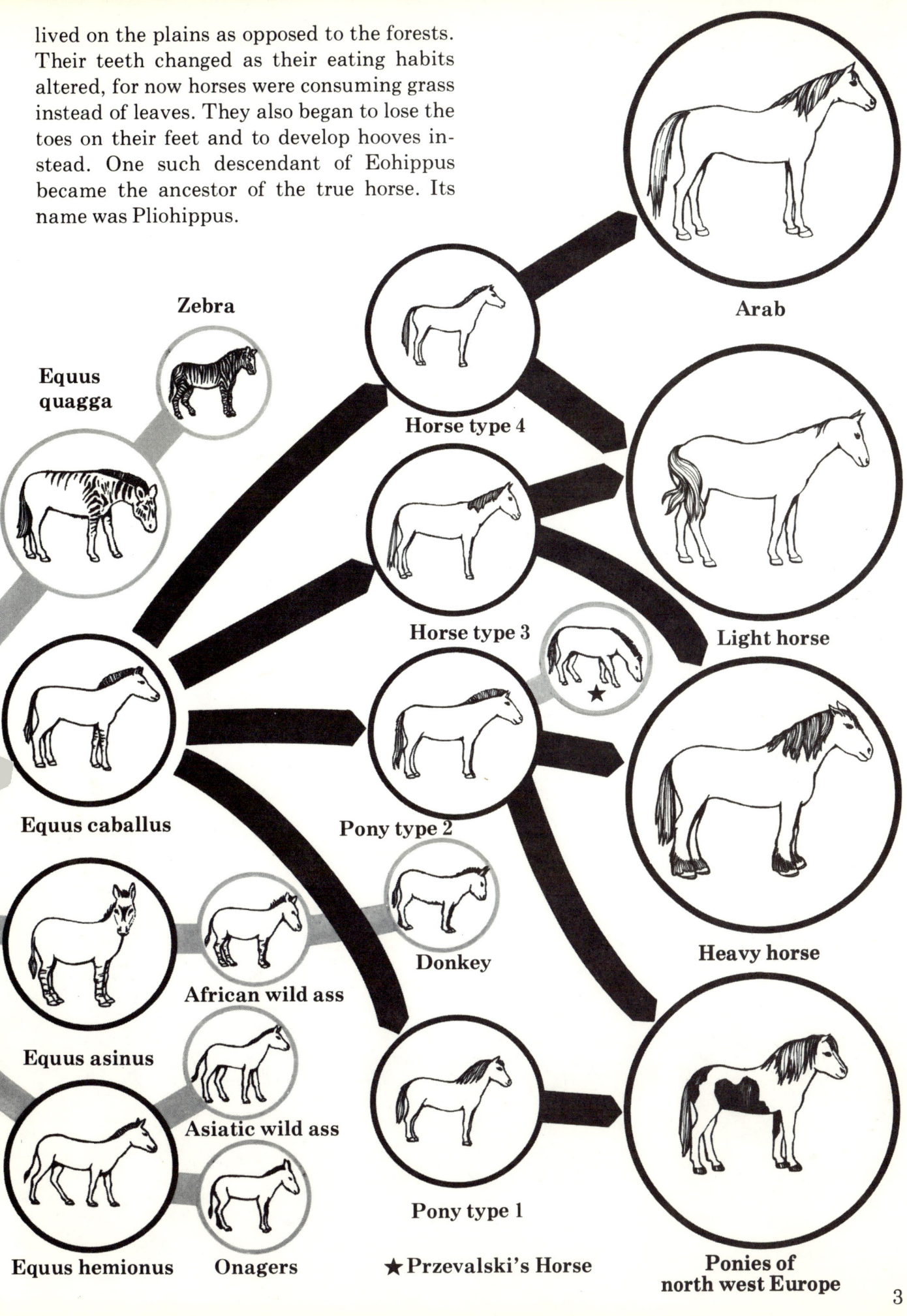

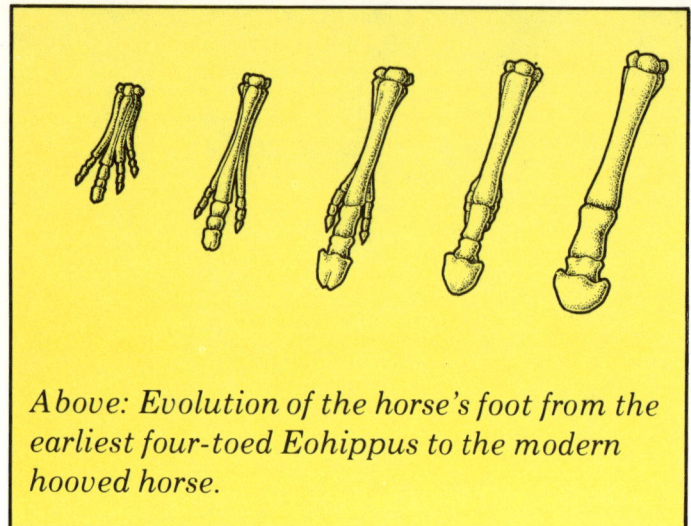

*Above: Evolution of the horse's foot from the earliest four-toed Eohippus to the modern hooved horse.*

# The Dawn Horse

The earliest pictures of horses, found mainly in caves in France and Spain, show us that prehistoric man regarded the horse as an animal to hunt and kill for food. Most of the paintings, which date from 30,000 to 10,000 B.C., show tough little ponies being struck by arrows. For Cro-Magnon man, the horse represented a source of food, clothing, and materials which could be made into tools.

It is not known definitely just when man ceased to kill horses for food and began to train them to help him in his way of life. Perhaps it happened as hunters drove bands of wild horses into fenced corrals only to remove one, on occasion, for food. With a variety of other game available, it may have seemed more sensible to keep the horses for other uses, even though early man had not yet considered how he could employ them.

During the next five thousand years, men began to settle on the land and form agricultural communities. The sowing and reaping of crops took its place as a source of food, along with hunting. Oxen were harnessed to plows and, later, although we do not know exactly when, horses began to replace the strong but slow oxen. It was the first attempt to involve horses in a working relationship with man.

As farmers gradually learned more about the horse, they started to experiment with feeding it, rather than expecting it to live solely off the land. They discovered that horses fed on grain grew much stronger than those given only grass. And when they began to dry out the summer grass to make hay to feed their animals during the long winter months, they took another step forward.

Clearly, at some stage, someone took the

*Above: A representation of horses by early man in the Lascaux caves of southern France. The paintings were discovered in 1940 by some young boys searching for their lost dog. Scientists have dated the paintings as being 20,000 years old.*

step of climbing onto a horse's back and trying to ride it, and it was not long before man discovered the advantages of riding over walking. Most importantly, it meant men could reach the hunting ground much faster than they had been able to on foot and, in their search for food, they could travel farther than ever before. It must also have become obvious that warriors on horseback were in a much stronger position than those who fought on foot.

*Below: Life for the "dawn horse," Eohippus, was often filled with dangerous moments. Here, a herd of Eohippus flee before a mighty Diatryma, a flightless, meat-eating bird.*

# Eastern Hordes

About two thousand years ago, it seems the nomadic peoples of Asia became restless and eager to leave their homelands. Perhaps it was because their crude farming methods and rather arid land could not support the sudden increase in their population, or maybe the climate changed and it grew too cold for them. All we know for certain is that in the first century A.D. there began the first of many migrations of people across Asia.

This movement began in the form of raiding parties. Across the Mongolian border, peaceful settlements in China suddenly found themselves under attack by the murderous Huns. Initially, the local populations were probably too surprised to protect themselves, but eventually, in desperation, they struck back and forced the invaders to retreat. Defeated, but not ready to give up, the Huns turned their attention toward the West.

Vast hordes of mounted tribesmen poured down from the Asiatic mountains and

*Below: Scene from a vase, showing ancient Greek horsemanship.*

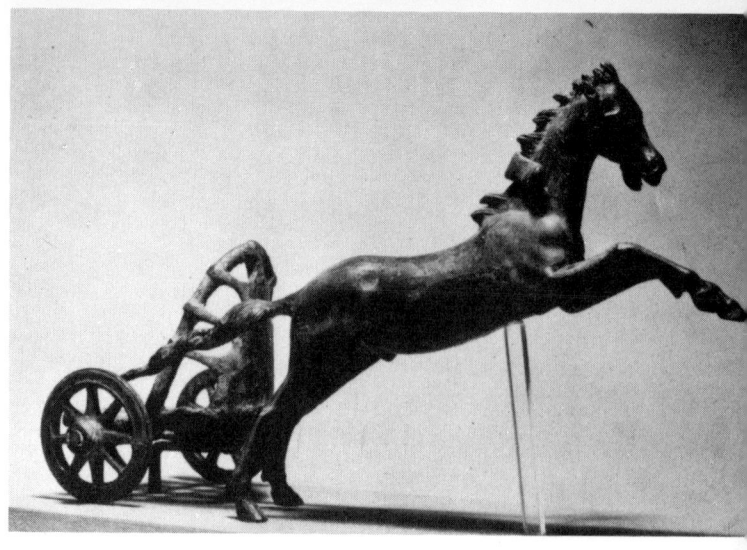

*Above: Model of a two-wheeled chariot, of the kind used by the Romans.*

stormed into Europe. They rode on tough little ponies, whose appearance had barely changed since the last Ice Age. The animals have since become known as Przevalski's Horse, named after Colonel Przevalski, who rediscovered these ponies sometime in the late nineteenth century.

Wave after wave of Avars, Sarmatians, Scythians, and Mongols ransacked their way through the settled lands of northern and eastern Europe. As they came, they pillaged, stole, killed, and burned. The natives fled before these strange and ferocious nomads of the East until the whole of Europe seemed to be on the move.

So far west did the barbarians travel that eventually they reached the gates of Rome. Mighty as Rome was at this time, the empire could not long resist the powerful invasions of the barbarians. In the end, the weakened empire collapsed and the hordes poured in, destroying and burning all they could not carry away and killing the inhabitants in a wild fury. The destruction of Rome marked the beginning of the Dark Ages, which were to last for many centuries.

How do we know all these things about the Eastern invaders and the defeated Romans? Most of our knowledge about the ancient world has come from fragments of writings, pieces of pottery, and remains of ancient buildings and cities. But the amazing discovery of the frozen tombs of Pazyryk has given us the most accurate picture ever found of the life of the nomadic tribes of the East during the centuries following the fall of the Roman Empire.

The tombs of Pazyryk belonged to Scythian chieftains and were built in a valley situated in the Altai mountains of southern Russia. Because of the high altitude and the peculiar construction of the tombs, the contents of the burial mounds froze, leaving them perfectly preserved. The Scythians were great horsemen and the tombs contained many horses, together with saddles, saddle cloths, bridles, driving harnesses, and ceremonial trappings.

Wagons were also found in the Pazyryk tombs, together with two different types of horse. Some were coarse ponies that had probably been used to pull the wagons, but others were larger and much finer horses, and these had probably been kept solely for riding.

In ancient times, one of the most traveled routes from the Middle East to China was the Silk Road. On the way it passed through the kingdom of Bactria, a small country in what is now the northern part of Afghanistan.

Merchants who had stayed in Bactria during their journey told the emperor of China about some wonderful horses they had seen. They called them "golden horses" because they seemed to have a golden sheen to their coats. Some even described them as "heavenly horses." These horses, they said, were far superior to the rough Chinese ponies. They were taller, swifter, finer, and more beautiful in every way. The emperor became determined to acquire some of these horses for himself and he sent messengers to the king of Bactria asking if he could purchase them. The king always refused.

The emperor sent a thousand gold pieces and the figure of a horse modeled in solid gold to the king, who seized the treasure and had the messengers executed.

This foolish action made the emperor of China furious, and he sent his army to besiege the Bactrian palace. The first attempt failed, but the second was so successful that the soldiers returned to China with thirty purebred golden horses and three thousand half-bred mares and stallions.

In 500 B.C., Sybaris was an ancient settlement in a fertile part of Italy. The people who lived there enjoyed a rich and comfortable life through very profitable trading pursuits. As in most early communities, horses were important to the inhabitants of Sybaris. They admired the animal's beauty and even taught their horses to dance to the strains of a lute, training them to pirouette and trot in place. But their dancing horses were to cause their downfall when a neighboring settlement, Crotonia, decided to make war on the Sybarites. Although the Crotonians knew that they would be heavily outnumbered, they had devised a cunning plan to defeat the soldiers of Sybaris. The Crotonian army included a number of musicians and, as the two armies faced each other, these musicians were ordered to play dance music. The Sybaritic horses immediately started to dance. Unable to fight properly, the Sybarites had no defense against the Crotonian cavalry, and they were overrun.

*Above: Chinese bronze horse made in* A.D. *200.*

*When knights began to wear heavy armor, they found it so cumbersome that they were unable to mount their horses unassisted. One solution was the winch.*

# Armed for Combat

A thousand years after the fall of Rome and the invasion of Europe by the Eastern hordes, the horse had become as important in warfare as the knight in his armor. Indeed, in times of war, a knight was expected to provide a horse and a number of men as evidence of his loyalty to the king.

By the time of the Crusades in the eleventh century, knights rode to war in lightweight, chain-mail armor and sat astride sprightly but powerful steeds. As they neared the enemy, they would charge forward at a gallop, with lances held horizontally in front of them. This was the sort of warfare for which the knights had long trained, and it required skilled horsemanship, rapid maneuvering, and tremendous bravery.

Gradually conditions changed. With the introduction of better-quality metals, swords and battle-axes could be made that were many times more powerful and damaging than weapons of earlier wars.

Yet it was really the invention of the longbow which led to the introduction of completely new tactics in war. Armed with this new weapon, archers could send a stream of arrows at the approaching enemy cavalry. Their shooting was not very accurate, but it did not matter because each archer could fire a great number of arrows in rapid succession. Those which missed the knights might well hit the horses, causing a cavalry charge to peter out almost before it had begun.

To protect both men and horses from the deadly longbow, plate armor was developed.

Made of metal, it covered the knight from head to toe. Except for its legs the horse was similarly covered. The armor was immensely heavy and very awkward, so much so that once a knight had been buckled into it he could hardly walk. A special type of crane had to be used to lift him into the saddle. If he or his horse fell, it was almost impossible for them to get up again.

The horses used were slow and heavy due to the tremendous combined weight of their own armor and their armored riders. Ponderous creatures, these animals were similar to today's cart horses.

As time progressed into the fourteenth and fifteenth centuries, warfare no longer gave the knights a chance to show how brave and dashing they could be. Impeded by their heavy armor, it was impossible for them to dash anywhere. In fact, they were more likely to die simply by falling off their horses rather than by facing a glorious death in the midst of battle.

Because of this, the idea of staging mock battles developed, while the real ones were left to paid foreign soldiers. Bands of knights would charge each other across an open field and fight as they had in the past, with lances and swords. Sometimes they were even killed. Most, however, lived to fight again another day.

*Below: As war became less glorious, knights turned to tournaments of mounted combat for excitement and adventure.*

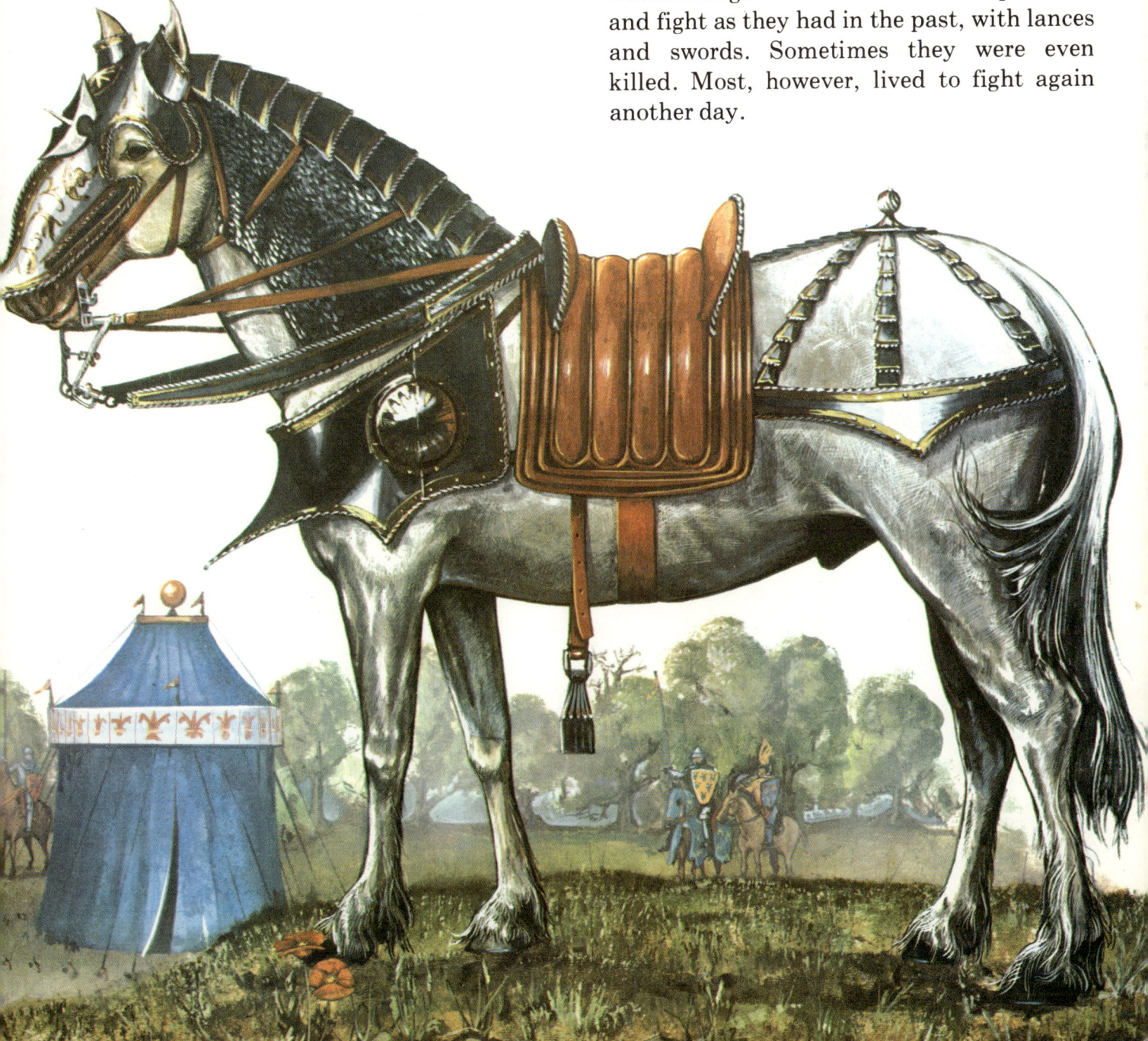

# Bred for Battle

Thousands of years before the Crusades, horses were used to pull war chariots. Two men rode in each chariot, one to drive the horse, and the other to fire arrows at the enemy. The ancient Assyrians and Egyptians fielded many squadrons of two-wheeled chariots in the battles they raged against their neighbors.

Chariots had a number of disadvantages. Although the opposing army was at first very frightened at the sight of the chariots bearing down upon them, they soon discovered that the vehicles could be stopped or made ineffective by hitting the horse, the driver, or even the archer with a rain of arrows.

A well-trained infantry learned to ignore the thunder of hooves and the war cries of the charioteers. Many foot soldiers were killed, of course, but there were always more, ready to send a deadly hail of arrows at the approaching chariots.

Julius Caesar first landed in Britain in 55 B.C. He thought that conquering Britain would be easy, for his troops were the best-trained in Europe. But he failed to make allowances for two things. The first was the weather in the English Channel; the second was the horsemanship of the Celtic bar-

*Below: Papyrus scene of ancient Egyptian war chariot and archer.*

barians who occupied southern England.

The few cavalry units that Caesar had included in his army failed to make a landing because the ships carrying the horses were blown off course by gales in the Channel. Instead, Caesar tried to land and wage war with only his foot soldiers.

**The Celts against the Romans**

The Celts were ready to face them, mounted on sturdy little ponies. They rode down to the beaches and poured wave upon wave of arrows into the Romans as they struggled ashore. Long before the legionnaires could assemble their weapons ashore, the Celts had galloped out of range and were preparing to charge Caesar's troops again.

The Celtic ponies were so surefooted and hardy that they had no difficulty in scrambling up and down the steep cliff paths, and they could gallop and wheel on the stony beaches without falling.

Caesar was forced to withdraw across the Channel. But the following year, he came again, this time with two thousand mounted soldiers in his army. Now his horses made all the difference, and he was successful in his conquests.

The most beautiful war-horses of all time were the Arabs. Today, Arab horses can be found all over the world and are highly prized for their beauty and strength.

Despite its small size, the Arab has great courage and staying power. This was very important in the warfare waged in the east, where mounted archers swooped on the enemy, fired their arrows, then turned swiftly away.

During the Crusades, when the English and German Christian soldiers traveled to the Holy Land in an attempt to regain the holy places of Palestine from the Saracens, they found that the kind of tactics they had

*Left: Mounted Japanese samurai archers preparing to enter battle.*

used in Europe met with less success.

These Christian knights wore armor and tried to fight in formation, using first the lance and then the sword. But the Saracens preferred to harass the enemy, attacking the flanks of the crusading army and then retreating out of range whenever the Europeans attempted to meet them in a frontal charge. The crusaders were unsure how to deal with this sort of attack and were defeated many times.

After the Crusades, jousting tournaments became a popular form of entertainment in Europe. Fully-armored knights on horseback charged each other aiming to splinter the opponent's lance or to unseat him.

There were two versions of the competition—to the death and for fun. But even when fighting to the death it was considered a disgraceful foul to injure an opponent's horse. At the moment of contact the horses were trained to veer away to the right and thus became known as destriers, from the Latin word *dextarius*, meaning right.

Good destriers were much prized by their owners and were never taken to war. Instead, the knights kept horses called coursers to carry them into battle.

*The Parthians were extremely skilled horsemen who lived more than two thousand years ago. They developed a technique of attack called the Parthian shot. After charging the enemy, they would suddenly turn and begin to retreat. As the enemy chased after them, the Parthians would turn around on their horses and, while galloping away, shoot a hail of arrows into the lines of the approaching enemy.*

*In the First World War, horses were used as cavalry mounts and for carrying supplies. But, despite the fact that they were rarely used in charges, many horses died in the conflict.*

# The Invaders

Christopher Columbus reached America in 1492, but it was left to his generals to overcome the native Indians and claim America for Spain. One of the most famous generals was Cortés, who landed in Mexico, captured Mexico City, and then moved southward to Honduras. The Spaniards relied on their horses to strike terror into the Indians, who had never before seen such amazing beasts. The Indians saw them as monsters that looked like stags without antlers, made a great noise, and chewed iron bars.

**Cortés and the Black Charger**

Cortés had a fine black charger, known as Morzillo, which is Spanish for "black." Morzillo was an Andalusian horse of great strength. It carried Cortés 500 miles (806.5 kilometers) across Mexico and took part in the battle to capture Mexico City. Though it was wounded several times, it managed to march most of the 1,000 miles (1,612.9 kilometers) on to Honduras.

Just before the end of the journey, however, Morzillo got a splinter lodged in its foot, forcing Cortés to leave it behind with some friendly Indians. The Spaniard never saw his horse again.

Nearly two hundred years later, missionaries visited this place. They found a huge temple containing the statue of a seated horse. They were told that this was the figure of a wonderful "god-beast" which had been left with their tribe many years before. The god-beast was Cortés's faithful charger.

At about the time that Cortés was making his way down the coast of Central

America, far away in Europe the whole strategy of using cavalry was being violently changed by the introduction of the musket.

Firearms, like the arrow before them, had the advantage of being able to inflict injury on a horseman long before he could reach the infantry. In the case of the musket, the range was actually quite considerable.

The cavalry's answer to this new danger was to arm the horseriders the way the infantry was: in other words, to provide the horseman with firearms. Cavalry generals trained their men to charge, fire their pistols, and then, as they got near the enemy, to draw their swords for close combat.

In the eighteenth century, Frederick of Prussia invented the "light artillery." These were lightweight guns — each drawn by six horses — that could be moved into position quickly and easily. The "galloping gunners" were so successful that soon the French and the British copied the idea.

Massed cavalry charges still took place in later wars but, as firearms improved, the killing of horses became more and more terrible. Hundreds of fine horses on both sides were killed at the battle of Waterloo.

Before long, army generals realized that horses were more useful for pulling field guns, carrying dispatch riders, and drawing supply wagons than for riding into battle.

*The "Charge of the Light Brigade" took place at Balaklava in the Crimean War in 1854. Through a misunderstanding, the brigade launched its charge directly toward the Russian guns. At the end of the action, 247 men and 497 horses lay dead.*

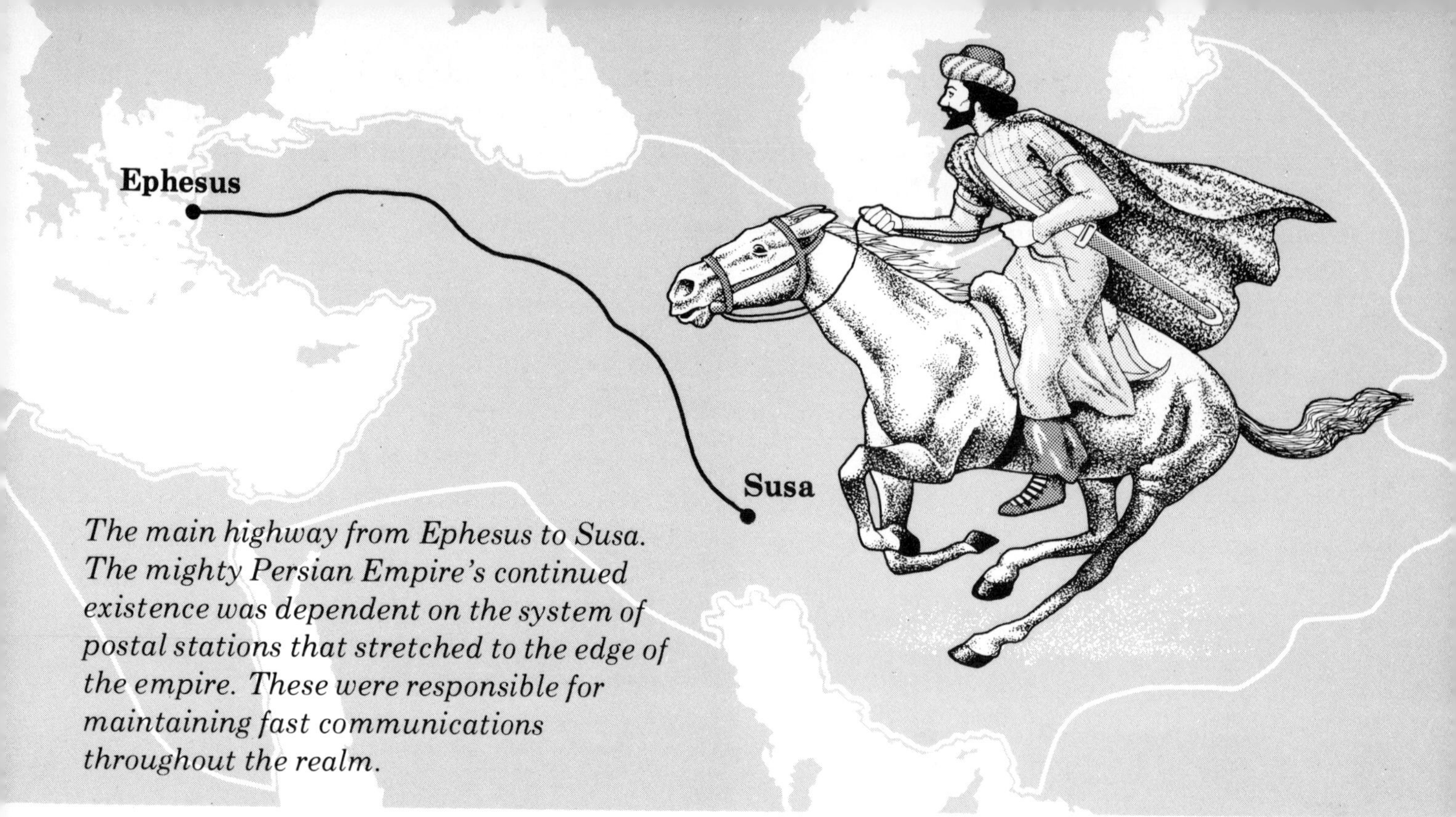

*The main highway from Ephesus to Susa. The mighty Persian Empire's continued existence was dependent on the system of postal stations that stretched to the edge of the empire. These were responsible for maintaining fast communications throughout the realm.*

# The First Mail Route in the World

The first postal system in the world was set up by King Cyrus of Persia in about 400 B.C. Throughout the Persian Empire, which stretched from the river Indus to Egypt, Cyrus arranged special routes along which were established posting stations. At each of these, men and horses waited to carry messages on to the next station.

Cyrus realized that a speedy, safe delivery was essential. For this, the messengers needed fit, fast, and reliable horses which could cover the distance between the posting stations in the quickest possible time without tiring. The best horses available were the golden horses of Bactria (see page 7), and Cyrus made certain that each station always had at least one or two Bactrian horses available for instant use.

Following Alexander, it was nearly one thousand years before anyone organized another horse-borne postal system. This was the Mongol emperor, Genghis Khan, who established posting stations all over his huge empire. They were only three miles (4.8 kilometers) apart in order that the post could be carried as quickly as possible.

**The first mail coach**

Any big city at eight o'clock on a summer morning is likely to be bustling with people going about their business. In London on August 8, 1784, however, there was a special feeling of excitement in the air, and crowds gathered near the General Post Office. They were

14

there to watch the departure of the world's first mail coach.

Several changes of horses and fifteen hours later, the packages of mail were safely delivered to the post office in Bristol. It was eleven o'clock at night. The London-bound coach was already seven hours out of Bristol and due to arrive at the capital at eight the next morning.

The opening of the new mail coach route was so successful that soon many other cities were demanding mail coaches from the Post Office. Over the following years, many fine carriage horses were imported from Ireland to pull the coaches over each stage of their various journeys.

The public was delighted with the new system. Letters arrived safe and on time, even though the regulation speed of the coaches was at first limited to only six miles (9.7 kilometers) per hour.

The coming of the railways in the middle of the nineteenth century brought the mail coach services to an end. Trains, with their much greater speeds, could carry letters far more cheaply and swiftly than several relays of horses, however fresh they were and ready to go. But for a long time afterward, horse-drawn vehicles continued to be used to deliver local mail, and even today, horses are used to carry mail in some parts of the world.

It was April 12, 1860. In Carson City,

*Left: A pony express rider about to leave a way-stage on a fresh horse. Right: "The mail must get through" was a tough motto that the riders followed in all conditions.*

Nevada, a young man named Warren Upson waited impatiently for the first mail pouch to be carried across America by the pony express. His sturdy pony was saddled and ready, waiting for the mail to arrive from the east.

Ten days earlier, Warren Upson had fought his way through the snow with the first westbound mail. Few people thought he would make it, but his pony was a tough little mustang which had tackled the snow drifts with the same grim determination as his rider. Now Warren Upson was prepared to repeat his journey.

Even before the incoming horse was jerked to a stop, its rider had vaulted to the ground and whipped the mochila (mailbag) from his saddle with one quick movement. Like lightning, Warren Upson hurled it over his own saddle, leaped onto his horse, and began to head west for the mountains.

The snow had stopped falling, but the drifts were still chest deep. Snow clung to his pony's legs. At one o'clock on April 13, he handed the mochila over to another pony express rider to make the last run to Sacramento.

Warren Upson was just one of the hundreds of young men who carried the mochila for the pony express between April

1860 and November 1861. The route covered 1,966 miles (3,170.9 kilometers) between St. Joseph, Missouri and Sacramento, California. The journey in either direction was scheduled to take exactly ten days.

The men and their ponies faced immense dangers. Hostile Indians shot at them with arrows. Swollen rivers had to be crossed. Sometimes the men had to battle through blinding rainstorms and other times they sweltered under a blazing desert sun.

But they upheld their motto, "The mail must go through," and thus made light of their difficulties.

# Behind the Team

During the time of the Roman Empire, roads in Europe were always kept in good condition. They were straight and well surfaced. Even long after the Romans had departed, traveling along them on horseback was fairly quick and comfortable. As the Dark Ages drew on, however, roads, like most other things, deteriorated, and by the late Middle Ages they were little better than tracks filled with muddy potholes in winter and deep ruts in summer.

To get from one place to another, most wealthy people traveled by horse. For others there were slow, heavy wagons, while the poorest people went on foot.

In the sixteenth century, a wheelwright living in the town of Kocs in Hungary, conceived an idea that was to revolutionize travel and, indirectly, the whole of European society. Yet what he did was so simple it was strange no one had thought of it earlier. Instead of making the wheels on a wagon all the same size, he put smaller ones on the front axle and larger ones behind. At the same time he also made the body lighter.

The effect of this simple change was immediate and dramatic. The new vehicles built in this way were faster, safer on the corners, and less tiring for the horses. They looked smarter and, for the first time, appealed to the wealthy as an alternative form of travel to horseback. Soon, everyone in Europe was clamoring to ride in the new "coaches" and, if possible, to own one.

With the tremendous popularity of this new mode of transportation came demands for better roads. In the eighteenth century, for the first time since the Roman influence, techniques of road construction were evolved and put into practice. Two great engineers, McAdam and Telford, built roads which were to last for the next two hundred years, until modern road technology would be developed in the twentieth century. With the new roads came improved coach services and the introduction of even faster coaches.

In America, the era of the stagecoach came long after its establishment in Europe, but when it arrived it was an instant success. People had long felt the need for a more comfortable means of long-distance travel, and by 1820, stagecoach lines were carrying mail and passengers between the midwest town of St. Louis and the East Coast.

The most famous stagecoach in America, the "Concord," offered a comfortable and fast ride. It was named after the town in New Hampshire, and its graceful, egg-shaped body swung on leather "thorough braces" between the axles.

Although there were many stagecoach lines operating out of California, there was no regular service operating right across the continent. Even though the gold rush had filled many pockets with riches, no one until the 1840s had tried to improve on the mule trains for the carriage of supplies, gold, and mail. In 1852, however, the coming of Wells, Fargo & Company changed this forever.

The longest stage route on record was the Butterfield Overland Mail, which was also the first mail and passenger service between San Francisco and St. Louis. At its peak, the Butterfield line needed eight hundred men to run it and was carrying more mail than the Pacific steamboats.

The man who was responsible for the mail and for the safety and comfort of the passengers was the stagecoach driver. His word was law. The seat next to the driver was the most prized on the coach and it was given either to the most important passenger being carried or, more usually, to an armed guard. This was because the coaches were often attacked by masked bandits or Indians. Stage drivers were expert at handling their teams of highly spirited horses, which they drove at a hard gallop even over the most difficult terrain. This was the only way they might hope to evade attacks by hostile bandits.

*Below: While the stagecoach provided a regular means of transportation, it also became the focus of attacks from outlaws and Indians.*

17

# The Willing Worker

Bearing soldiers in warfare and pulling coaches and wagons are only two of the ways in which horses have patiently served man over the centuries. Through the ages, horses have been employed in a host of different ways. From threshing grain on the land to hauling coal deep underground, the horse has proved itself to be a remarkably willing worker. Horses have been harnessed to grinding machines and forced to turn the central shaft by plodding patiently around the perimeter. They have labored in front of the plow, worked in mines, carried huge packs over mountain passes, and allowed themselves to be dressed up for ceremonial occasions. Man's progress on this earth would have been very different without the help of the horse.

We still use the term *"horsepower"* to describe the power of an engine, even though horses as a source of energy have almost completely disappeared from the industrial scene. The term *"horsepower"* originally referred to the number of horses which were needed to pull a steam engine when it was taken from place to place.

*Horses at work in the city streets of the nineteenth century — pulling a fire engine, a stagecoach, a cart, and a hansom cab.*

Before the development of the steam engine, the strength of the horse was needed to operate all sorts of machinery in many different fields. Many children today have never seen a horse working on a farm, yet two generations ago the farm horse was a common sight. Heavy and muscular, with strong, shaggy legs and a large kind head, it pulled the plow and the threshing machine, brought the hay and corn home from the fields, and was used for any other hauling jobs the farmer might require.

Horse-drawn boats

Canals were built to link natural waterways and to make it possible to carry great loads by boat from one side of the country to the other. The boats used for this purpose are known as barges. In the days when canals were regularly used for transportation, engines had not been invented and horses were used instead to haul the barges through the water.

Every canal was built with a towpath alongside it. The barge horse was harnessed to the barge and walked along the towpath, pulling the barge as it went. When the barge reached a lock, where the level of the canal changed, the horse would have to be unhitched, led to the other side of the lock, and rehitched to the barge after it had passed through.

It was, of course, a very slow method of travel, but also a peaceful one, and the life of a barge horse seemed a contented one. In modern times, the use of machines has meant that ponies are no longer needed to work in coal mines. During the last century, however, large numbers of ponies spent their working lives deep underground. All sorts of ponies were used in the mines, and Shetlands were very popular because they were small but strong.

The ponies were usually stabled underground in big caves hewn out of the rock. Once a year they would be given a vacation above ground and would have a chance to roll on the grass and scamper about in the sunshine.

Before the invention of the internal combustion engine, city streets were filled with horse-drawn vehicles. In a big city, traffic

*Above: Tireless workers. An eighteenth century Flemish print of Belgian horses on a threshing machine.*

jams were just as frequent as they are today, but a century ago, instead of the noise of horns and engines, there was the clatter of hooves and the jangling of harnesses.

Bus and tram horses worked the hardest. There were no fixed bus stops, as there are today, and buses had to stop whenever they were hailed.

# At Work and On Guard

The western world has progressed considerably since the days when horses were made to haul heavy loads or to operate machinery. Today, horses have been replaced by the internal combustion engine. But the horse is still highly valued in remote or mountainous regions where people are too poor to own wheeled conveyances, or where trails are impassable.

In many hilly districts, horses are better able to cope with steep slopes than are tractors. And, in cattle ranching or sheep rearing, the horse is still the best means of inspecting or rounding up vast herds of cattle and flocks of sheep.

Still, horses will sometimes be seen in places where you least expect them. In London, for example, many breweries still employ horses to deliver beer to public houses. The pub building may be of a very modern design, but the beer could arrive in a huge dray pulled by two heavy horses, just as it has for two hundred years.

## Festivals and fantasias

All over the world, horses still have a part to play in ceremonies and festivals. In Morocco, regular festivities are held in which Arab tribesmen take part. They are called fantasias, and they provide the opportunity for a marvelous display of skilled and daring horsemanship.

The tribesmen put on traditional dress

*Horses have long been harnessed to plows and carts. Once domesticated, the draft horse's patient nature is perfectly suited to laborious work, and despite its immense strength, it is almost always docile and gentle. Below: Clydesdale in cart harness. The traditional horse brasses date from very early times. They were originally devised as magic charms to ward off evil spirits which would harm the horse.*

and groom their Arab and Barb horses until they shine, decorating them with ribbons and braid. Then they are ready to take part in a ceremonial parade, mounted games, or headlong gallops. There is always a great deal of shouting and discharging of firearms.

The ceremonies which take place in England are quieter and perhaps more serious, but they are still very colorful. The most famous of all is the ceremony of Trooping the Color, which takes place at the time of the queen's official birthday in June. Every year, the queen goes to Horse Guards Parade in London and takes the salute, while the flag of one of the guards regiments is carried past her. Afterward, there is a display of marching to the music of one of the regimental bands.

One of the most impressive sights is the parade of the mounted guards as they wheel in formation across the parade ground, first at a walk and then at a slow trot. All the horses behave perfectly, but none more so than the police horse on which the queen herself is mounted, which has to stand still throughout the whole ceremony.

One of the most moving ceremonies in recent years in which horses were involved was the funeral of President John F. Kennedy, assassinated in 1963. Adhering to a tradition which stretches back to ancient times, it was decided that the gun carriage bearing his coffin would be followed to the cemetery by a riderless, although saddled and bridled, horse. The horse chosen for the ceremony was an army charger called Black Jack, picked for its magnificent appearance. The choice almost proved a disaster, for the crowds, the white lines on the roads, and the slow pace of the procession frightened the horse so much that it took all its handler's strength to prevent it from galloping away. On the other hand, it may also be true that the horse's wild white rimmed eyes and sweating flanks added to the drama of the occasion as its fury contrasted with the stillness of the crowds.

*Above: Brewer's dray being pulled by a matched pair of Shire horses. Shires, the biggest horses in the world, often reach a height of 18 hands. Yet for all their immense size, they are very gentle and peaceful. In England, Shires take part in the annual farm horse presentation awards.*

"We get our man"

The Royal Canadian Mounted Police no longer use horses in their everyday work. Helicopters, airplanes, Land Rovers fitted with two-way radios, and police dogs are the modern methods of enabling the Mounties to "get their man." Nevertheless, the Mounties have enough horses to deserve their name.

*Below: The mounted bodyguard of a Nigerian emir in full ceremonial dress.*

# Inside the Horse

Both ponies and horses can be a variety of colors. The colors can be "whole colors," which means they are the same all over, or "broken colors," which are mixtures of colors. There are eight basic whole-color patterns: bay, which is the color of a ripe horse chestnut with a black mane and tail and black legs from the knees down; black, which must include a black muzzle; brown, which is actually dark brown to black with a tan muzzle; dun, a sort of sandy brown, believed to be the original color of all primitive horses; chestnut, a reddish color of many different shadings; cream, a very light chestnut with similar mane and tail; palomino, a pale gold; and gray, which varies from dark gray to white, either with or without dappling.

Roan is one of the broken colors, consisting of any one of the whole colors mixed with hairs of another color, as in blue roan and strawberry roan. Piebald is white and black in patches, and skewbald is white and any other color in patches. (Horses of these last two colors are also known as pintos or American paints.) Spotted or Appaloosa are white with various spots of different colors.

Markings are extra marks which help in identifying ponies. The main ones are called black points (black lower legs) and stockings or socks (white lower legs).

Baby horses are called foals. A male foal is a colt; a female is a filly. When a foal reaches its first birthday, it is a yearling.

After a mare has given birth to a foal, she licks it all over. This helps to clean and dry the new baby and also gets its blood to circulate properly.

A mare usually has one foal at a time, although occasionally twins are born. Gray or white horses are born black. Their coats gradually change color as they grow older.

A foal can stagger to its feet within an hour of its birth, and within four to six hours a foal can walk, although shakily at first. Almost as soon as it is born, a foal can focus its eyes and, within a week or so, it cuts its first teeth.

Horses and ponies are fully grown at about three to four years old. Generally speaking, this is the age at which they can begin being trained to carry a rider. This training is called breaking in. Racehorses are broken in when they are two years old, which means they are still very young. Special care therefore is needed in their training. A child's pony should not be broken in until it is at least four.

Horses are considered to be in their prime between the ages of seven and fifteen.

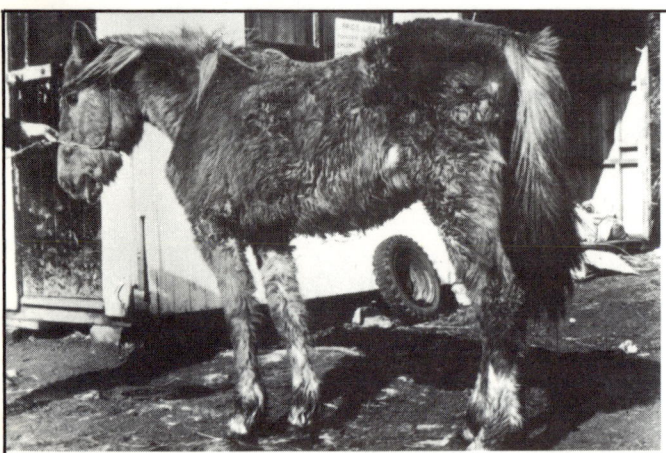

*The two photographs above show very clearly the differences between a horse in an unhealthy condition and a horse which is healthy.*

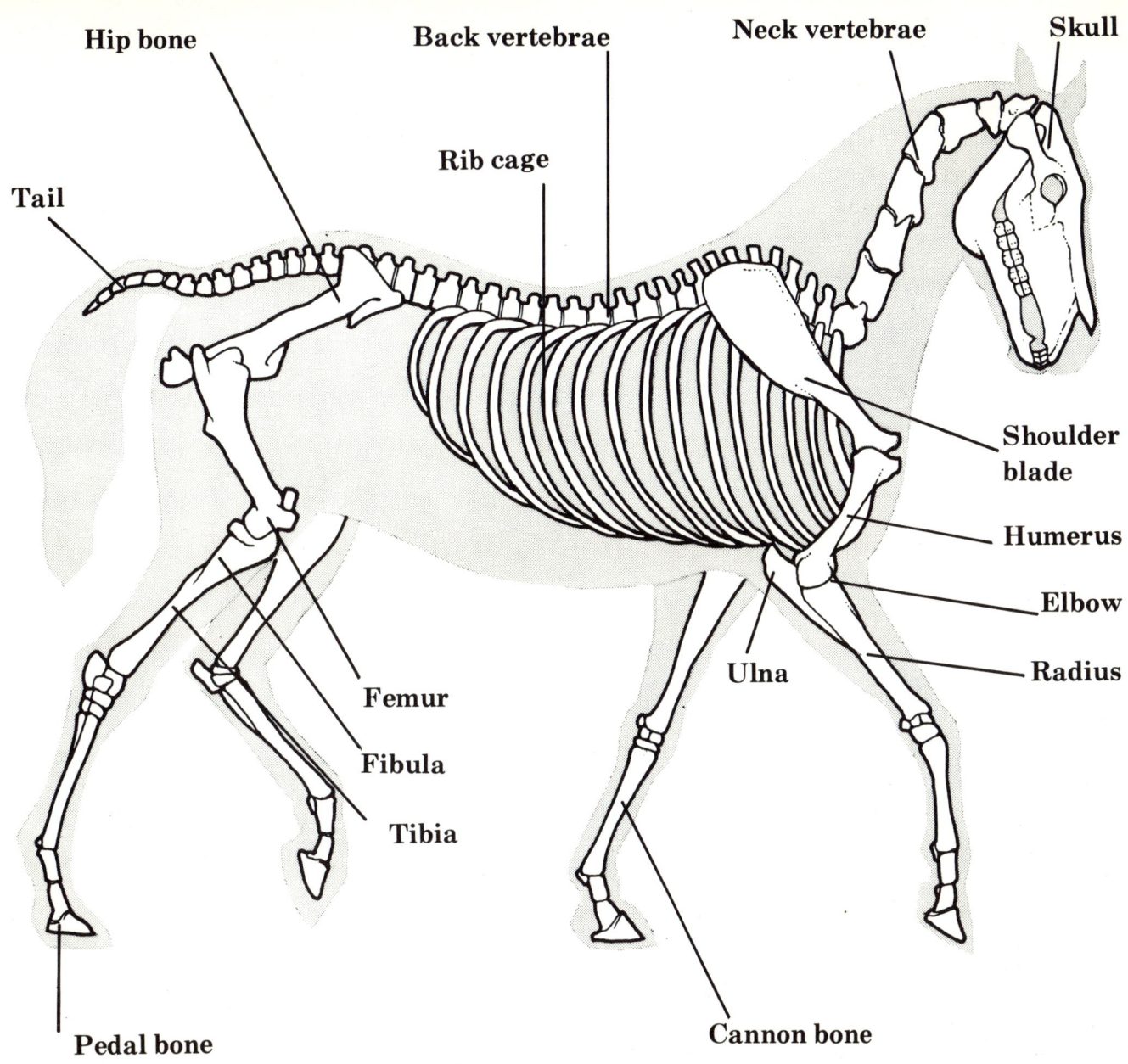

A horse over twenty is quite old, but nevertheless, many horses continue a full working life well after this age. A few are still fit for work at thirty and over. The greatest known age ever reached by a horse is sixty two, attained by "Old Billy," an English barge horse.

As horses get old, they display many of the same aging characteristics as humans. Their coat may go quite white in places, particularly around the head, and they move more slowly as their joints tend to become stiff and gnarled.

Like all animals, horses can become ill, but they can also be protected against various dangerous infections.

Equine influenza can be guarded against by a course of injections. Tetanus or lockjaw, which is a poisoning of the nervous system, may develop if a horse has a deep cut or wound and is not treated with anti-tetanus injections. It usually proves fatal.

A horse's legs are particularly liable to injury. Compared with the rest of it, the legs are very slender and fragile, especially when you consider how much weight they have to bear. Bad knocks, cuts, or sprains are common injuries.

A horse is a warm-blooded creature made up of a bony framework (the skeleton) which protects the vital organs and is controlled by muscles.

# Breeds of the World

There are more than 350 different breeds of horses and ponies in the world. They range from the tiny Falabella pony of Argentina, which reaches only 28 inches (71.7 centimeters) in height, to the huge Shire horse of Great Britain, which is over 17 hands tall.

Men wanted big, strong horses to do hauling work and help on the land so the draft horse was developed. There are several kinds of draft horse, but the proudest and the showiest of them all is the French-bred Percheron.

The Percheron has Arab blood in its ancestry. Any horse with Arab blood has a special quality. It walks along with its head and tail held high and a look in its eye which seems to say, "I am the best in the world."

Men wanted to ride and teach their children to ride, but the horses were too big.

*Above: View of the famous Cadre Noir School in France where only first-rate stallions are trained.*

*Below: The Percheron, a heavy farm horse, first bred in Le Perche, France.*

Of course, children can learn on any type of horse, provided it is calm. But it is more sensible for a beginner to learn on a pony that is not too large. For a suitable type, men looked to the north, where the climate and terrain tended to produce animals which were small in height but tough and hardy.

**Early riding techniques**

In Europe in the sixteenth and the seventeenth centuries, a special riding technique was developed. It involved training the horses to perform difficult but controlled movements at the slightest signal from their riders. These movements included trotting in place, spectacular leaps and kickbacks, pirouettes in one place, or diagonal movements across the arena. The technique was called *haute ecole* or high-school work.

The horse most suited for this type of riding is the Lipizzaner. The Lipizzaner is the famous breed of white horse used in the Spanish Riding School of Vienna. It developed as a cross between the Kladruber and a local breed, with a later mixture of Arab blood.

The horses were first bred at Lipizza, near Trieste, then in Austria, and were used as harness horses for the imperial carriages. Ever since then they have been used by the Spanish Riding School. They are very intelligent and docile animals.

**The acrobats' favorite**

Until recent times, acrobats who performed their acts on horseback liked to use horses that had a beautiful and striking appearance. The most colorful horse for this purpose was the Knabstrup, which originally came from Denmark and, unfortunately, is rarely seen nowadays. It had a broad back and a distinctive spotted coat. It is an old breed, which originated from another Danish breed, the Fredericksborg. The purebred Knabstrup is now almost extinct, but the strange, spotted coloring still appears from time to time on crossbred horses.

Britain has more native ponies than any country in the world. There are nine separate breeds in the British Isles alone. One of the most beautiful is the Welsh mountain pony, born and bred in the Welsh hills for hundreds of years. It still runs wild in the same hills.

*The Danish Knabstrup is favored by acrobats for its beauty and striking appearance. The breed is almost extinct, but its strange colorings can still be seen on crossbreeds.*

# The Specialists

If all your life were spent on a hill farm in Norway, your daily work would be made much easier if you owned a Fjord pony. This sturdy, strongly built pony is able and willing to tackle any task. It can help to plow steeply sloping fields, pick its way up narrow mountain paths, move logs, and carry packs through swift mountain streams. Yet it is gentle enough to take the children to school or the farmer's wife to market. In snowy weather, it can plunge through deep drifts and its thick coat protects it against the cold.

The Fjord pony is usually a dun color and has a coarse mane which is usually carefully trimmed to make the hairs stand up straight. From the side, the upright mane gives the neck a strongly arched look.

Chariot racing was a popular sport in ancient times. The horses which took part in these races thundered around the track at full gallop. This was quite different from modern harness racing, in which the horses are not allowed to move out of a trot. This may sound slow, but in fact the trot carries them over the ground at tremendous speeds.

Trotting races are popular in America, the Soviet Union, and various countries in Europe. Breeds of horses have been produced which will trot very fast without breaking into a canter or gallop. One of the most successful was bred by Count Orlov of

*Left: The Norwegian Fjord pony is perfectly suited to life in the hard, northern winters. It is also strong and gentle.*

Russia. Two hundred years ago, he mated an Arab stallion with a Dutch mare, and the offspring and its descendants became known as Orlov Trotters.

In England, travelers frequently express amazement at the way sheep dogs round up sheep; the dogs seem to understand the sheep. In America, the horses used by cowboys to herd cattle have a similar understanding of their job.

A good cowpony acts by instinct. It knows how to bring a stray steer back to the herd and how to separate a calf from the rest of the cattle. When its rider lassos a steer, the horse will stop immediately and throw its weight back to keep the rope taut.

*The Holstein, a German breed, is considered ideal for show jumping because of its strong hindquarters, intelligence, and courage.*

The breed usually ridden by cowboys in their work is the Quarter Horse. It is descended from the horses brought from Europe by pioneers who used to race them over a quarter-mile (402.3 meter) distance.

Men have always admired horses which are particularly striking in appearance. One of the oldest breeds in the world is the Friesian horse, which comes from Friesland in

The Netherlands. It is always jet black in color, and in the days of horse-drawn transportation, it was very popular for pulling hearses. The Friesian is a strong, muscular horse which holds its head high and lifts up its feet well. In the Netherlands, it can often be seen at horse shows where matched teams of Friesians draw carriages driven by Dutch couples dressed in national costumes.

Show jumping as a sport has been practiced for less than a hundred years. As it grew more and more popular, there was a need for a horse which could jump well and enjoy doing this as much as its rider.

In Germany, it was found that the Holstein was just the right sort of horse. Its strong hindquarters give it tremendous thrust as it takes off over a jump, and it is able to tuck in its forelegs to avoid knocking the jump down. Best of all, it has great intelligence and quickly learns to judge the approach to even the highest obstacles.

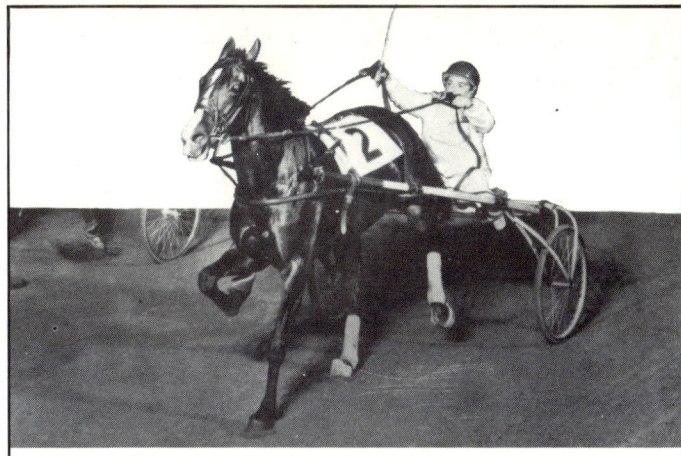

*Trotting races enjoy great popularity in the United States and in various countries in Europe. Among the best horses for this sport are the Russian-bred Orlov Trotters.*

*Below: The breed most preferred by cowboys for ranch-work and cattle herding is the Quarter Horse.*

27

# Power and Speed

The fastest breed of horse in the world is the English Thoroughbred. It can gallop at more than 43 miles (69.2 kilometers) per hour.

Racing today is an international sport, and racehorses are raised in studs all over the world. They all have to be entered in the General Stud Book, which was started in England in 1793, and all Thoroughbreds can trace their ancestry to one of the three Arabian stallions brought to England nearly three hundred years ago.

The oldest of the three is the Byerly Turk, which was captured from the Turks during a siege and brought to England by Captain Byerly, who used it as a war horse.

The Darley Arabian was born in 1702 and imported to England by a Mr. Darley of Yorkshire. Among its descendants have been some of the greatest racehorses ever known.

*Above: The Thoroughbred is a direct descendant of the Arab, from which it derives both its tremendous stamina and its speed.*

*The Arab profile is unique among purebred horses. The front of the head is curved inward, giving it a "dish-faced" appearance.*

The Godolphin Arabian was pulling a cart in Paris when it was discovered and brought to England in 1730.

The Arab, the ancestor of many breeds of horse, has been raised in the Nejd Plateau of central Arabia for nearly two thousand years. It did not originate in Arabia, but came from the north, in the areas now known as Iran (Persia) and Russian Turkestan. The Arab peoples have been very careful about keeping the breed pure. No horse was accepted into a pedigree unless it was purebred. This is how the name of its western descendant, the Thoroughbred, was derived.

The pure Arab is marked with some unique points. The front of its short, wide head curves inward so it is "dish-faced," and it has large eyes. In the backbone, between the last of the ribs and the croup, it has five bones instead of six like other breeds. This gives the Arab its short, "well-ribbed-up" appearance. It also has fewer bones in the tail, having sixteen instead of eighteen. This causes the well-known gay, high carriage of the tail. The height is usually 13 to 14.2 hands (52 to 58 inches — 132.1 to 148.7 centimeters), and the Arab was the finest breed in the world until the development of the Thoroughbred.

Speed is not always the most valuable quality in a horse. In mountainous regions, where sudden changes of weather are also common, the presence of a hardy, trustworthy pack pony can make the difference between life and death. Small wonder that Italian hill farmers value the Avelignese breed so highly. These tough ponies are so surefooted they can carry their packs over the steepest mountain ranges. Bad weather never worries them, and they are unbothered by sudden precipices.

Some horses are bred primarily for riding, while others may be bred specifically for harness work. In Finland, the most popular horse is one which will undertake any job. It is called the Finnish Universal and it appears to possess many of the good points of other horses. It is strong and muscular, enabling it to pull heavy weights. It is lively and fast, so that it is a pleasure to ride and can also be used in races and sport. Yet its even temper makes it popular with children.

*Below: The Italian Avelignese, a tough pony highly favored by the hill farmers because of its incredible surefootedness. The Avelignese is believed to be a descendant of the Tyrolese breed, an Austrian mountain pony.*

*Above: Finnish Universals enjoying a day's freedom in the fields. A strong and muscular horse, the Universal is used for hauling, is ridden in national races, and was once employed as a cab horse in Leningrad.*

# World of Riding

In seventeenth-century western European countries, riding was considered a particularly important art. The riding master was part of a nobleman's household and he taught the children of the house to ride, just as the dancing master taught them to dance, the tutor or governess gave them their lessons, and the fencing master taught the boys swordsmanship.

Unfortunately, the style of riding then in fashion was very boring. Small boys had to spend hours in the riding school learning to keep their ponies under tight control. They rode with very long stirrups and a tight rein, so that the ponies had to keep their necks well arched. This meant that the pony's weight was thrown back on its hind legs, even when it trotted and cantered.

The boys were dressed in tight breeches and velvet jackets, and they knew there would be trouble if their lace ruffles were torn or soiled! Most of the boys longed to take their ponies outside into the fields and woods where they could tear along, running races against each other and jumping fallen logs and low hedges. This sort of freedom was only permitted very occasionally.

In eastern Europe, on the other hand, horsemen were taught from an early age to ride as naturally as possible, keeping their knees bent and giving their horses a free rein. They knew that riding with stiff, straight legs and sitting back in the saddle meant that the horse was unable to move forward very easily. It was not until the twentieth

*Above: Shorter stirrups and bent knees characterize the riding style used in Europe.*

century that horsemen all over the world began to copy their method and style of riding.

If you look at pictures painted more than a century ago of western European riders, you can see how different they look from photographs of riders today. The old horsemen were riding with the backward seat. Their stirrups were long, and when their horses took a jump they leaned far back in the saddle. Unlike the eastern Europeans, westerners rode in a very stiff and formal way.

At the beginning of this century, an Italian cavalry instructor named Federico Caprilli taught his pupils a new method of riding. He told them to sit farther forward in the saddle and to ride with bent knees. He said that horses should be allowed to stretch their necks if they wished and all riding should be as natural as possible. Everyone laughed at Caprilli and his ideas, but he went on with his method of riding. At the 1907 International Horse Show the show-

*Left: American Indians used to ride bareback and guide their horses with their legs. Right: A South American gaucho.*

*Above: The western style of riding.*

jumping team entered by the Italian cavalry won their events with such ease that Caprilli's style of riding began to be copied by most European horsemen. It forms the basis of all riding techniques taught today.

Wherever a horse has to travel many miles in a day, it is the "cowboy" or western style of riding that has been found to be most comfortable for both horse and rider. The rider is helped by the comfortable western saddle, with its high pommel at the front, the deep, back-sloping seat, and the high back. He keeps his stirrups long and his legs almost straight. In this way, he is less likely to shift about in the saddle, so neither he nor his mount gets saddle sore.

# How to Ride

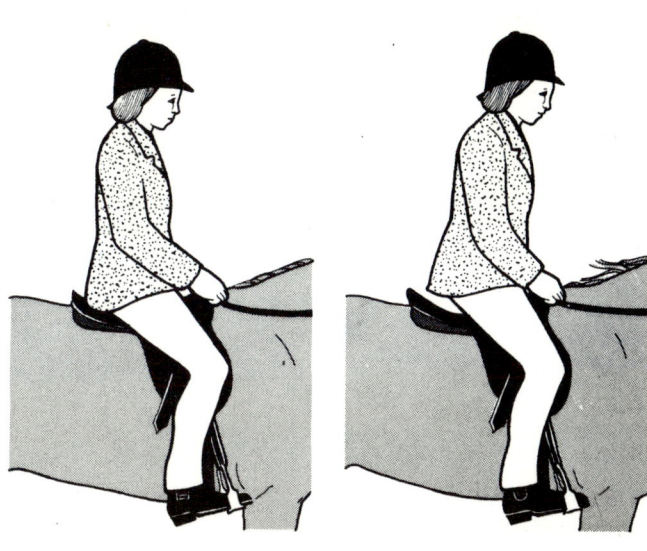

*When walking, sit well down in the saddle with your back straight, your head up, and your knees and thighs pressed against the saddle. The lower part of your leg is straight and free. To change to trotting, keep the same position, but apply more pressure with the lower part of your legs.*

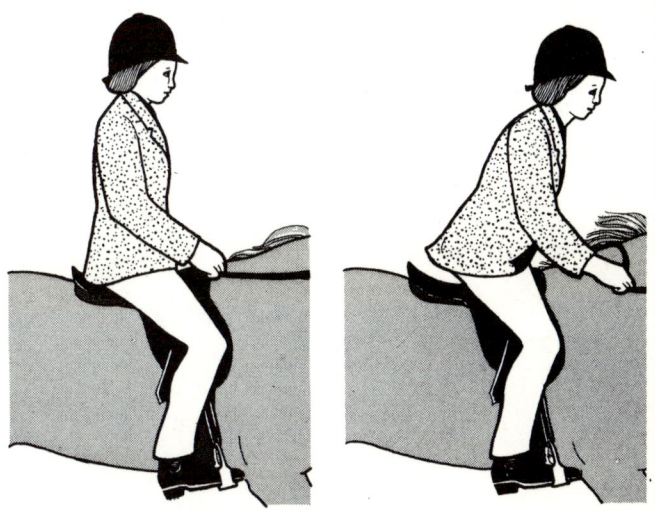

*To canter, sit down in the saddle so that you are doing a sitting trot. Then, increase the pressure of your lower legs just behind the girth. Do not lean forward. In the gallop, lean slightly forward and hold the reins a little farther forward than usual.*

# Taming the Wild

One of the most important things to learn about riding a horse is how to establish a means of communication between rider and mount. This means learning the correct system of signals and the technique for transmitting them to the horse. Everyone knows that you can kick or whip a horse to make it "go forward" and pull up on the reins to make it stop, but these methods of command are based on fear and pain, not understanding. Ultimately they will be ineffective.

The secret of good horsemanship, then, is cooperation between rider and horse, so that the rider gives the correct commands and the horse understands the significance of each instruction as it is received. It is only when communication has been established, on both sides, that a rider can begin to consider its purpose — to make the horse feel comfortable at all paces and in all conditions and to be obedient to the will of the rider. For most amateurs this is likely to be as far as they will want to go. But for more serious riders, there are far more advanced objec-

*Below: It takes many years of patient and hard work to train a horse for circus work.*

*One of the most exciting events in a modern rodeo is bareback riding, when a cowboy tries to stay on a bucking horse for up to ten seconds. Although this is only done today to thrill the crowds, it has its origins in the methods used by the old-time cowboys to break in their horses.*
*A herd of wild horses would be rounded up and driven into a high-fenced paddock called a corral. The cowboy chose his horse, roped it, and tied it, kicking and plunging, to the fence. Then he put a saddle on its back and fastened the girth. Using just a rope halter around the horse's nose, the cowboy leaped on its back and released it into an empty paddock.*
*The horse, of course, did everything it could to get rid of its rider. It bucked and reared, rubbed along the fence, and even got down on the ground and rolled over from side to side. Only the most experienced cowboys could manage to break in their horses.*

tives, such as dressage, show jumping, and horse trials.

On a very basic level, there are two main teaching methods used in Europe, termed the German and the Italian. The German method is based on the classical approach, which evolved during the Middle Ages and the Renaissance, and is today best seen in the methods of the Spanish Riding School.

The Italian system, sometimes called the Caprilli system after Captain Caprilli, is much freer in approach, placing more emphasis on letting the horse find its own balance without strict obedience.

When a young horse is old enough to be broken in, its trainer begins by teaching it to accept a bit in its mouth. The next stage is known as lungeing. The horse has a long rein attached to its bridle, and the trainer encourages it to move around in a large circle, the trainer himself acting as the pivot. All the time, the teacher gives the horse words of command, such as, "Walk," "Trot," "Halt." Lungeing exercises are very important because they help to improve a horse's balance, build up its muscles, condition young horses before subjecting them to a rider's weight, calm down a spirited horse, and teach a horse the habit of obedience.

Later, a saddle is put on its back, and, for a while, the horse does its lessons with the saddle on and perhaps the stirrups hanging down to get it used to the feel of them against its sides.

Finally, the trainer leans over the horse's back and takes his feet off the ground. For the first time, the pupil experiences the weight of a rider.

The most important factor in all training is the relationship between pupil and teacher. As long as the horse has learned to trust its master, it will not be afraid to try whatever it is asked to do.

It is hard to understand sometimes how horses in the past ever did anything demanded of them. Although the ancient Greeks believed that kindness was the best method of teaching, some of the later trainers were very cruel indeed.

A very famous Italian horseman called Grisone, who lived in the sixteenth century, published a book on horsemanship. In it he advised trainers to shout at the horse, "with a terrible voice and beat him yourself with a good stick upon the head, between the ears."

*Below: In lungeing, the trainer begins the work of teaching the horse to obey commands.*

# Horse Sense

The care and attention given to keeping a pony's coat and body clean and in good condition is called grooming. Regular, careful grooming not only makes a pony look well cared for, but it also helps to keep it healthy as it stimulates the pony's skin, muscles, and blood circulation. The time spent in grooming a pony is also an essential part of getting rider and mount to know and trust one another.

If a pony is kept out at grass, thorough grooming is not so important as if he is stable-kept. In fact, the coat of a grass-fed pony should not be brushed too much, as this will remove the essential grease needed to keep it warm and dry. Ponies kept in a stable, however, should be given a complete grooming every day

The necessary pieces of grooming equipment are three types of brush, two combs (one for the mane and one, called a curry comb, for cleaning the body brush), a hay wisp for massaging the pony's skin, a sponge to wash the pony's eyes and head, a stable rubber (similar to a linen drying cloth) and a hoof pick which, as its name suggests, is used for removing dirt from the pony's hooves.

Grooming begins with the pony's head. The head should be brushed very gently with the body brush, and then the eyes and nose must be carefully cleaned with a sponge. Next, using the body brush, the neck is brushed with long, downward strokes. The strokes should always follow the direction of the hair, but avoid banging the brush against the body. The whole body should be groomed with the body brush, starting at the highest point and then gradually working downward. After five or six strokes, draw the brush through the curry comb to remove particles of dirt. Then groom the legs, brushing from the top downward.

Using the body brush, brush the mane on the side where it lies naturally. Take a lock and brush it gently to remove all tangles. Then dampen it with the water brush so it lies down.

Hold the tail in your left hand and, with the body brush, pull a few strands of hair away from the rest. Brush this to remove all tangles and then brush down another section of hair, continuing until you have brushed the entire tail.

All four feet must be picked out with a

*Giving a horse the right food in the correct quantities is extremely important. The main staple of the diet is hay, but it is also necessary to vary the diet with oats, barley, beans, green food, and lots of water.*

*Horseshoes of the past. Left: A Greek Hipposandal ("Hippo" in Greek means "horse") and, right, a Japanese plaited straw shoe, attached to the hoof by thongs.*

hoof pick. To do this, run your hand down each leg in turn and lift it by supporting the fetlock joint. Work from the heel to the toe so that you do not hurt the frog. Ponies kept at grass need to have their heads groomed and their feet picked out. Then all they need is a brush-over with the dandy brush.

Grooming is only one part of general horse care. Another concerns where and how they live. As mentioned already, some horses are kept in stables; others, especially ponies, will live happily in a field.

Even until fairly recently, many houses in England were built with a stable or two attached. You can still see many of these, with the stable converted into a garage. The stable was the place where the owner kept his harness pony or carriage horse. Big houses had room for several horses in the stables.

Stable-kept horses need a lot of care and attention, including daily exercise. If an owner has a limited amount of time to spare,

*Regular and careful grooming is important to keep your pony healthy.*

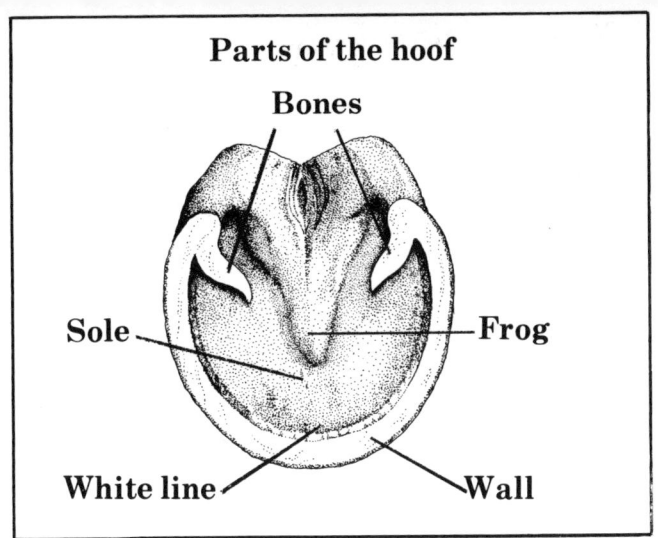

Parts of the hoof

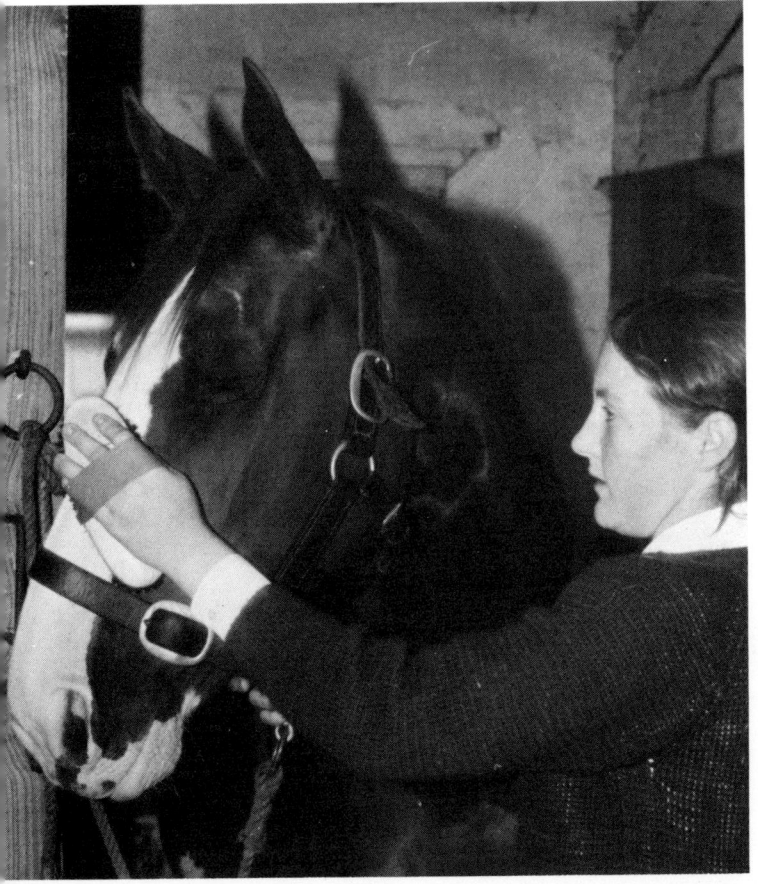

he will probably choose to keep his horse or pony in a field.

Sometimes people are concerned that a field-kept pony has no roof over its head to protect it in bad weather. However, as long as it has some form of windbreak, such as a high hedge or the side of a building, it will be all right. Even a hollow in the ground gives shelter from a gale.

In winter, ponies need extra food, especially hay. Nature provides them with a thick coat to keep them warm and a layer of grease on the skin to keep them waterproof. Protected in this way, they do not mind cold rain and snow. In summer, they like to find a shady spot in the field. Here, they will stand for hours, head to tail, lazily flicking flies from each other's faces with their tails.

In hot countries, where dirt roads are baked by the sun, a horse's hoof is very hard. The horny surface of the hoof wears down evenly and rarely breaks. A horse in such conditions has no need of a horseshoe to protect its feet.

In the moister climates, however, the horn of the hoof is much softer. When the horse has to do a lot of work on hard roads, the hoof is liable to break or split. To protect it, it is fitted with an iron shoe.

# Saddling Up

Using a bit in a horse's mouth to control it goes back three thousand years. The first bits hardly differed from those in use today. Basically each was a piece of metal linked in the center to make it bend, and fitted with a ring at each end.

In general, a bit will not hurt a horse, unless it is given a sudden tug. A good horseman always tries to be very gentle with his horse and tries to avoid pulling sharply on the reins.

The object of the bit is to assist the rider in directing the horse and regulating its pace, as well as to position the horse's head correctly. It is not for giving the horse violent commands to change direction; it is, rather, an invitation to cooperate.

### Early halters and bridles

The ancient Assyrians used to tie a thong around the horse's lower jaw when they wanted to just lead it along. They used more elaborate bridles when they rode or drove horses with their legs.

American Indians, however, used jaw halters even when they were riding. They would gallop bareback across the plains, guiding the horses with their legs. These halters were made of strips of buffalo hide, plaited to make them stronger. It was the girls' job to make the thongs, and then the boys went out to catch the wild horses and break them for riding.

Some bits used in the past have been very cruel. Many were fitted with spikes and, if roughly used, would stick into a horse's mouth and make it bleed. Much depended, however, on the skill of the rider. A sympathetic rider with "good" hands could use even a spiked bit without hurting the horse in any way whatsoever.

### Riding without saddles

A modern saddle is designed to rest on the horse's back on either side of the backbone, so that it does not rub the horse's back and cause sores. To lift it clear of the spine, it has an inner framework called a tree.

Thousands of years ago, people did not know how to make this support. Instead, they stuffed two cushions with grass or wool and joined them together with a piece of leather or cloth. Sometimes no saddle at all was used. Instead a piece of blanket was simply thrown over the horse's back for the rider to sit on.

*Below: There are many different types of bit, mostly designed to help the rider control his horse. Left: The jointed snaffle, which acts upward on the corners of the lips when the head is held low. Right: The Pelham, which basically combines the snaffle and the curb in one bit.*

**English saddle**

*Above:* A saddle used in western riding is bigger and heavier than an English saddle. Its size means that the weight of the rider is carried over a greater area of the horse's back. For riding over long distances this is far more comfortable for the horse. The horn on the front of the cowboy's saddle is used to attach the lariat. Broad stirrups, usually made of wood, protect the rider's feet from such things as cactus thorns. They are hung from wide sweat flaps, which guard the cowboy's legs from his horse's sweating sides. The English saddle allows the rider to sit in the closest possible contact with his horse and in no way hinders the application of the rider's legs in his control of the horse.

## Leaping to Fame

For a sport that is only just under a hundred years old, show jumping has grown rapidly in popularity, both in respect to those taking part and as a spectator sport. In the United States, the New York International at Madison Square Garden is one of the highlights of the show jumping season. In Germany, show jumping ranks second only to soccer in popularity; and in Britain, millions of viewers watch their television sets every evening during such events as the Royal International and the equally popular Horse of the Year shows.

There are many reasons for the popularity of this sport, one of which is that the combination of man and horse looks very appealing on film. The sport is also very easy to understand and to follow. And, perhaps most important, it is a sport that builds up to a climax, the actual winner being unknown until the last horse has jumped.

Up to the late 1800s, riding schools almost ignored the teaching of any jumping techniques. Hunting men took up jumping when fields became increasingly divided by hedges and fences. These "obstacles" had to be jumped if the riders were to keep up with the hunt.

Basically, show jumping can be divided into three types of competition: those that take place against the clock; those that test jumping ability, but with the clock brought in for a jump-off at the end; and those that are purely tests of jumping over great heights, time not being a factor.

Speed competitions are designed to test how well a horse is handled, as well as its obedience, training, and jumping ability. This is why the fences jumped are often easier and lower than in other competitions. The results are judged on the basis of the number of penalty faults acquired by each

*Left: The Belgian rider, P. Weier, takes his horse over a fence at the Cardiff show jumping competition in 1975.*

horse. The horse with the least faults wins. In time-fault judging, each fault is counted as a certain number of seconds, so the rider with the fewest faults is also the quickest to cover the course.

In the old days of show jumping, the rules were so difficult that few people bothered to follow the sport. But now it is much easier both to watch and to judge.

*Below: Johan Heins, a Dutch rider, showing fine horsemanship and control.*

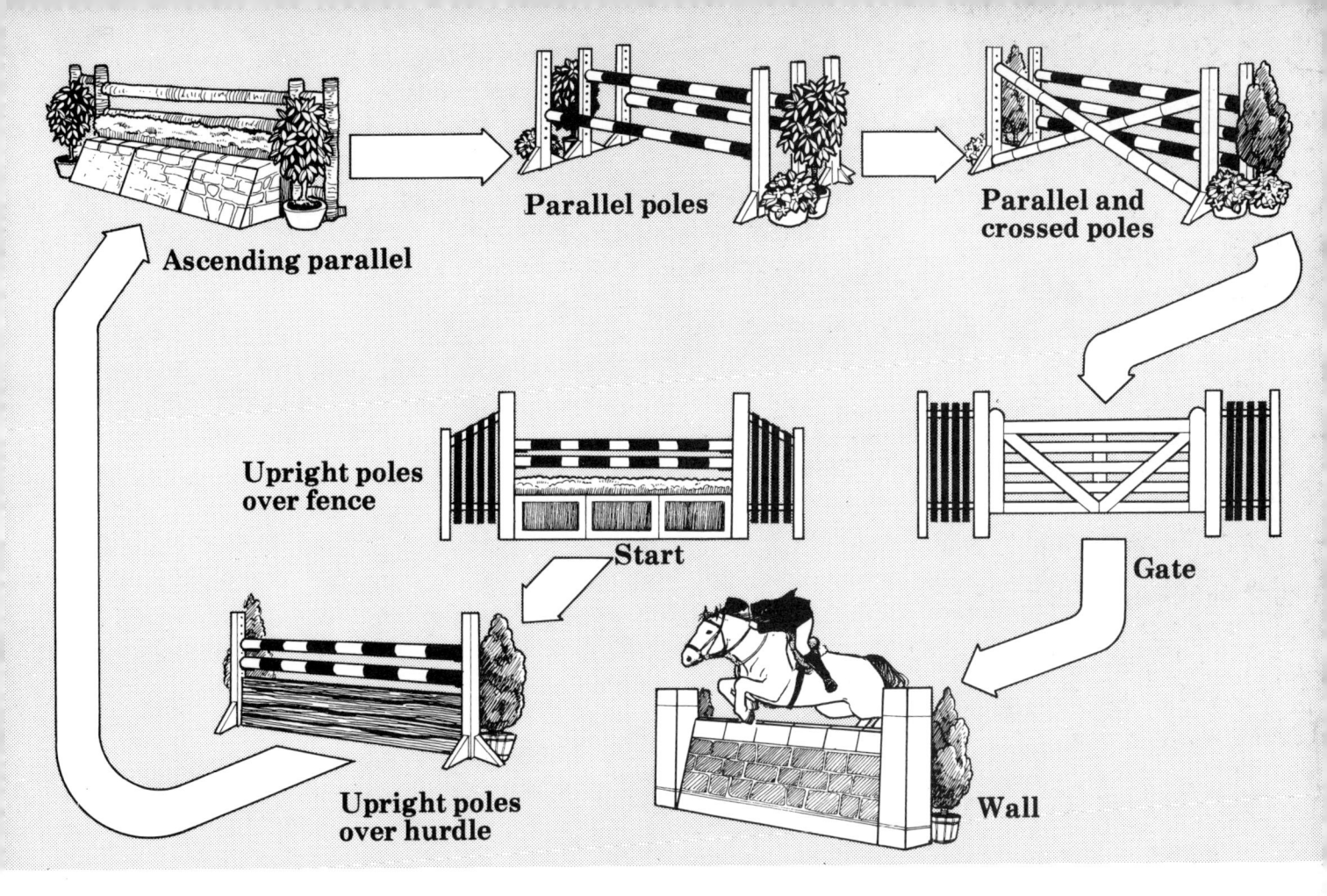

Many people who ordinarily are not interested in horses find themselves fascinated by show jumping events.

The most important international competitions are the team events known as the Prix des Nations, or Nations Cups. In Europe, each country has only one Nations Cup, held at the official International Horse Show. The United States and Canada may stage two competitions.

Individual teams consist of four riders and horses, each jumping the same course twice. The score of the best three in each round counts toward the final total. When this event first began, there were only three riders on each team, so all the scores were counted in the final total. Now, if one rider does badly, his team still has a chance.

The international show jumping event which captures the whole world's interest is the Grand Prix des Nations Cup, the Olympics. National teams from many countries compete against each other for team and

*Above: A typical layout for a show jumping course. The jumps are designed to test the horses in many different ways.*

individual gold, silver, and bronze medals. Other show jumping competitions include the men's and women's European championships and the men's world championships.

A well-trained show jumping horse is one that, besides possessing jumping ability and a love of the sport, has three important qualities. These are balance at all times, complete obedience to the rider's wishes (since the time spent between fences might mean the difference between winning and losing), and impulsion. Impulsion is not, as many people imagine, the same as speed. It is more like a clockwork spring, the releasing of which enables a horse to come to a big fence at an awkward angle and yet clear it; or to jump faultlessly through a combination, the fences of which may be at different and awkward distances from each other.

# Games Horses Play

Imagine galloping into a thundering crowd of horsemen in order to snatch the body of a goat which one of the other riders carries between his knee and saddle. You might well wonder how you and your horse would ever manage to survive.

Yet *Buzkashi*, as goat-snatching is called, is played regularly in Afghanistan. There seems to be no limit to the number of players, and no rules. All the spectators can see is a cloud of dust; all they can hear is the snorting of horses and the wild shouts of the riders. The game is always played at top speed, yet seldom does the horse or rider get hurt.

A similar sort of game is played in the Argentine. Called *Pato*, it uses a dead chicken instead of a goat. The one who snatches the bird is the winner, and his "prize" is to roast the chicken and serve it to his fellow players.

Many mounted games call for great courage on the part of the rider. In the Argentine, the gauchos, or cowboys, take part in a sport called *Domade*. It is rather like the bronco busting of American rodeos. The gauchos have to ride wild horses from the pampas for as long as they can. Needless to say, there are many spills!

*A bats le Sultan* is a Russian game which is equally fast and furious. Riders wear fencing masks covered with feathers, and carry extremely sharp swords. With these they try to cut away the feathers from their opponents' masks.

In Turkey, there are javelin games in which teams hurl light, blunted spears at one another, hoping to score three hits and win the game. These javelin games go right back to ancient times, when spears were first used for hunting.

There were many Englishmen living in India in the nineteenth century. Some worked for the government, others served in the Indian Army, and many were planters on the great tea estates in Assam.

It was the tea planters who "discovered" polo. This ancient game had flourished in the East for centuries but it was quite unknown to westerners. The English tea planters thought it was tremendous fun. At first, like the local players, they rode tiny Manipuri ponies. They were so small that the planters'

*Below: Pigsticking in nineteenth century India. This was a fast and dangerous sport.*

*Below:* The modern game of polo was very popular in the nineteenth century among tea planters in India.

*Above:* A breathtaking moment in a game of Buzkashi. *This sport, which is still played in Afghanistan, involves trying to snatch a goat away from another rider at top speed.*

feet could almost touch the ground, but the ponies made up in toughness and agility what they lacked in height.

Polo soon became popular with the rest of the British residents in India, and from there it spread to other parts of the British Empire. It also became very popular in the Argentine and in the United States. Today, the Argentine has the best polo players in the world, and most of the best polo ponies are Argentinian. Many polo ponies now have some Thoroughbred blood in their veins.

Alexander the Great played polo and so did his archenemy, King Darius of Persia. It was played in China and Mongolia, too. In Japan, rules stated that players had to get up to twelve balls into a goal situated in the center of the field. The modern game has a goal at either end of the field.

41

# Thunder on the Turf

Racing is a sport with a long history. Bareback riding is recorded as being very popular in ancient Greece. Certainly the Romans were passionately involved in all sorts of horse racing, especially the chariot racing which was organized in the arenas of every provincial city, as well as in the mighty Colosseum of Rome.

**Horses for the high jump**

In many countries in medieval Europe, war horses were often given their head in races across the tournament fields. At horse fairs, small boys would entertain their elders by jumping onto horses and racing against each other for small prizes.

Organized racing, as such, did not begin until the reign of King James I of England, in the seventeenth century. From that time onward all English kings and queens, except the "puritanical" Queen Victoria, have been enthusiastic race goers.

Steeplechasing is a race with jumps set up around a course. It started in Ireland in 1752, when two gentlemen raced their horses

*Below: Starting gates ensure that all the horses in a race start at exactly the same time and from the same line.*

*Taking a high fence during Britain's 1965 Grand National, in which Jay Trump, the favorite, pounded to victory.*

against one another from one church steeple to another. For a long time, all races were cross-country, using a prominent church steeple as the finishing post.

There are records of steeplechases being held late at night, with riders dressed in nightcaps and nightshirts urging on their horses across fields and over gates and hedges. The only light was that provided by the moon.

Later, as steeplechasing became more popular and organized, special race tracks were established. Artificial fences were used instead of the farmers' gates and hedges.

If you love horses, even if you have never learned to ride, it is possible to get a job as a trainee jockey. The most important qualification is your size. Apprentice jockeys must be small and weigh around 90 pounds (40.8 kilograms) or less.

An apprentice is employed by a

racehorse trainer. He lives at a racing stable and helps to look after the racehorses, grooming, feeding, and exercising them. A boy who works hard and shows promise may eventually get a chance to ride in a race, probably a special one for apprentices. Not all boys become successful jockeys, of course, but for those who do succeed, the prospects are glittering.

In the early days of English racing, jockeys rode with very long stirrups and sat upright in the saddle. This was the style of riding generally practiced. About a century ago, however, an American jockey named Tod Sloan went to England to ride. He amazed everyone by drawing his stirrup leathers up several holes so that his knees seemed to be tucked under his chin. Then he crouched low over his horse's neck during a race. "Like a monkey on a stick," was how people scornfully described him. But Tod Sloan kept on winning races and, before long, other jockeys copied his style. Today, all flat-race jockeys ride with very short stirrup leathers.

# Quiz

Please read the whole book before attempting to answer the questions.

1. What was the "dawn horse"?

2. What are the smallest and what are the largest horses in the world?

3. Which was the most famous war-horse of ancient times?

4. What breed of horse is used by the Spanish Court Riding School in Vienna?

5. How many breeds of horse are there in the world?

6. What is a Thoroughbred?

7. Name a horse with spots.

8. Who brought the horse back to America?

9. What was a horse "brass"?

10. What was the Byerly Turk?

11. Where is the fetlock on a horse?

12. What is a filly?

13. How are horses measured?

14. Where was the game of polo first played and by whom?

15. How did the Greek soldiers manage to enter the legendary city of Troy?

16. Name the three special qualities of a show jumping horse?

Answers to these questions will be found on Page 47.

# Horse Tales

When people could neither read nor write, stories were handed down from generation to generation by word of mouth.

There were many stories about the centaurs, who were imaginary beings with the head and shoulders of a man and the body and legs of a horse. The ancient Greeks told all sorts of stories about them. The idea of a centaur is sometimes believed to have evolved from the nomadic tribesmen of central Asia who spent most of their time on horseback. A legend grew up that these beings were strange creatures — half-man and half-horse.

The most famous horse from Greek mythology is Pegasus, a wonderful creature with wings sprouting from his back. He was said to be the son of Medusa, the Gorgon, and Poseidon, the god of the sea. The only human to ever ride Pegasus was a man called Bellerophon. He caught the horse with a golden bridle and rode him to kill the Chimera, another legendary creature which was part lion, part serpent, and part goat.

Afterward Bellerophon tried to climb to the heavens on Pegasus's back, but the gods could not allow this and made him fall. Pegasus, however, flew on to carry the thunder and lightning of Zeus, the father of the gods.

Another horse of legendary fame is the

*Above: The mythical centaur, half man, half horse, was a creation of ancient peoples who had never before seen a horse and believed the rider and the animal to be one beast.*

*Below: The unicorn, the legendary "one-horned" horse, was supposed to have magical powers.*

unicorn, which means "one-horned." The unicorn was said to be a horse with a single horn sprouting from its forehead. It was supposed to be very savage, and there are many stories of how people tried to catch a unicorn. If they succeeded, it was supposed to bring them good luck.

Legend tells us that the best way to catch a unicorn was to stand in front of a tree while the unicorn charged, and then to step aside at the last moment. The unicorn, unable to stop, would bury its horn deep in the tree trunk.

The most famous war-horse of ancient times was Bucephalus, which belonged to Alexander the Great of Macedonia. Bucephalus is a Greek word meaning "ox head," and some historians say that the horse's forehead and face had a white star and a blaze in the shape of an ox's head, hence its name.

Everyone agrees, however, that the horse was both beautiful and spirited. Alexander is supposed to have been about twelve years old when he first saw Bucephalus in his father's royal stables. The horse was thought to be unridable, because it threw everyone who clambered on its back. Alexander believed he knew the reason and begged his father to let him try the horse.

Reluctantly, King Philip agreed. All the courtiers laughed at Alexander, but the boy went quietly up to Bucephalus and turned the horse's head toward the sun. He had noticed that the horse was afraid of its own shadow. Once it could no longer see its shadow, it quieted down. Alexander was able to ride it through the stable and out into the fields beyond. The boy's father was astonished and told his son to seek out a larger kingdom, for Macedonia was not big enough for one with such wisdom.

Thereafter, Alexander rode Bucephalus whenever he could. When, eleven years later, the young man set out to conquer the neighboring kingdoms, Bucephalus was his charger. It was always Bucephalus which carried Alexander into battle.

At last, in India, Bucephalus was badly wounded at the battle of the Hydaspes. Although bleeding from dozens of spear and javelin cuts, it carried its master safely out of the thick of the fighting before it collapsed and died.

*Below: The legendary conquest of Troy by a wooden horse. It was supposed to have been filled with Greek soldiers who waited inside until the horse was brought into the city. Then, under cover of darkness, they left the horse and attacked the guards in the town.*

# Glossary

**Agricultural show** A show where farm animals, machinery, and produce are on display and can be bought and sold. There is also a variety of competitions.

**Anvil** An iron block on which a blacksmith hammers and shapes the horseshoes.

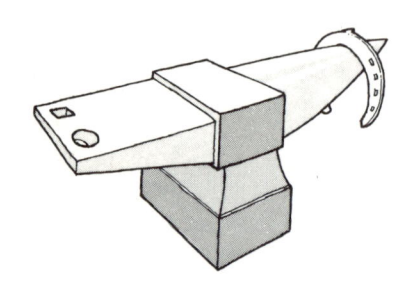

**Arena** A large space or stage on which sports or entertainments are performed.

**Breed** A family of horses that have the same general characteristics. For example the Thoroughbred is a breed of horse, the American Saddle horse is another breed.

**Canter** The natural paces of a horse are the walk, the trot, the canter, and the gallop. When a horse canters it moves in a moderate gallop.

**Carcass** The dead body of an animal.

**Cavalry** The mounted troops of an army. The strength of the cavalry in battle was its ability to attack at speed and so surprise the enemy.

**Crusade** A religious war waged against the Muslims by the Christians in order to recover the Holy Land. There were many Crusades and they lasted from 1096 until 1291.

**Curry** A wooden-handled metal comb which is used to clean the body brush after the pony has been groomed.

**Dray** A low cart without sides, often used by brewers for carrying heavy loads. A dray is drawn by large, powerful horses.

**Dressage** A test of the horse's training and of his obedience to the rider. Marks are given for each movement in the test and any stiffness and lack of response are heavily penalized by the judges.

**Forge** A hearth used by a blacksmith for heating metal to make it soft and workable.

**Frog** The v-shaped, fleshy part of a horse's foot.

**Hobble** A loop of rope tied to a horse's fetlock to prevent it from straying.

**Infantry** Troops who march and maneuver on foot and carry small arms.

**Javelin** A light spear thrown with the hand.

**Jockey** A professional horse-rider in races.

**Joust** To take part in mock battle in a tournament.

**Lance** A weapon consisting of a long wooden shaft with a metal head. It was used by a horseman charging at full speed.

**Lariat** A Mexican or South American lasso made of rope.

**Lasso** A long rope of leather with a noose at the end used for catching either cattle or wild horses.

**Lock** A part of a canal shut off above and below by folding gates. Sluices in the gates allow water in and out so that boats can be raised or lowered from one level of a river to another.

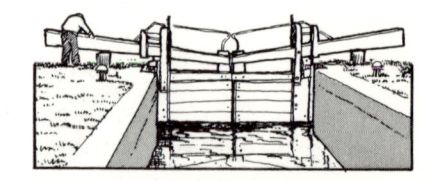

**Longbow** A bow drawn by hand in order to discharge a long arrow.

**Nomad** A person who moves from place to place to find new pasture for his grazing animals. A nomad usually belongs to a tribe of nomads.

**Olympic Games** The biggest sporting event in the world. Amateurs from over 100 nations take part. The games take place every four years and were started by the ancient Greeks.

**Pack-horse** A horse that is used for carrying packs or bundles of goods.

**Pampas** The vast treeless grasslands south of the Amazon River in South America. There is too little rainfall on these plains to allow trees to grow.

**Pirouette** A turn made by a horse in a dance without changing its ground.

**Pitch** An area of ground which is marked out for a team sport.

**Pithead** A group of buildings at the surface of a coal mine. From the pithead the miners enter the mine by going down in elevators.

**Pony Express** A postal system in the mid-19th century. Men on horse-back raced across the wild country of the West determined that "the mail must go through."

**Posting station** A place along the route of the mail coach where the horses could be changed.

**Prance** To walk in a succession of springing movements.

**Primeval** The first age of the world. Something which is primeval is so old it happened long before history was recorded.

**Quarry** An animal being chased by another animal is the chasing animal's quarry.

**Rack** A top-speed version of the slow gait. The rack makes an exciting end to a horse's performance in a dressage event.

**Rasp** To scrape or rub with a rough instrument such as a blacksmith's file.

**Retreat** To draw back. An army would retreat from a stronger army or after a serious defeat.

**Slow gait** A prancing movement in which each foot hesitates for a split second in the air just before hitting the ground.

**Stable** A building where a horse lives. A stable is fitted with stalls, loose boxes, rack and manger.

**Stage coach** A coach that carried passengers daily or on certain days on a regular route with several organized stops or "stages".

**Stud** A place where stallions for breeding are kept.

**Tactics** When a military commander spreads his troops out in order of battle, he is using tactics.

**Tournament** Tournaments first began in the Middle Ages. They were highly organized mock battles between knights. The events usually took place outside a town and were attended by many spectators.

---

Answers to Quiz on Page 43.

1. Eohippus. 2. Falabella and Shire. 3. Bucephalus. 4. Lipizzaner. 5. 350. 6. Thoroughbreds are descendants of pure-bred Arabians. 7. Knabstrup. 8. Cortez. 9. To ward off evil spirits. 10. One of the three original Arabian horses brought to England 300 years ago. 11. Withers are the forward part of the back and the fetlock is the joint above the ankle. 12. Female foal. 13. In 'hands'. 14. By Indian natives. 15. By hiding inside a wooden horse and 16. Balance, obedience and impulsion.

# Index

**Abats le Sultan** 40/41
**Afghanistan** 6/7, 40/41
**Aging** 22/23
**Alexander the Great** 40/41, 44/45
**Arab Horses** 10/11, 28/29
**Argentina** 24/25, 40/41
**Armor** 8/9
**Assyrians** 10/11, 36/37
**Avelignese** 28/29

**Bactria** 6/7, 14/15
**Barge horses** 18/19
**Bellerophon** 44/45
**Bits** 36/37
**Black Jack** 20/21
**Breeds of horses** 24/25, 26/27, 28/29
**British ponies** 24/25
**Bucephalus** 44/45
**Butterfield Overland Mail** 16/17
**Buzkashi** 40/41

**Cadre Noir School** 24/25
**Caprilli, Federico** 30/31, 32/33
**Cavalry** 8/9, 12/13
**Celts** 10/11
**Ceremonies, horses in** 20/21
**Charge of the Light Brigade** 12/13
**Chariots** 6/7, 10/11, 26/27, 42/43
**China** 6/7, 40/41
**Clydesdales** 20/21
**Coach, invention of** 16/17
**Coloring of horses** 22/23
**Cortés, Hernando** 12/13
**Cowboys** 26/27, 30/31
**Crusades** 8/9, 10/11
**Cyrus, King of Persia** 14/15

**Dark Ages** 6/7, 16/17
**Diseases** 22/23
**Dray horses** 20/21

**Egyptians** 10/11
**English Thoroughbred** 28/29
**Eohippus** 2/3, 4/5

**Falabella pony** 24/25
**Finnish Universal** 28/29
**Fjord pony** 26/27
**Frederick of Prussia** 8/9
**Friesian horse** 26/27

**Gaits** 30/31
**Gauchos** 30/31, 40/41
**Genghis Khan** 14/15
**Grisone** 32/33
**Grooming** 34/35

**'Haute ecole'** 24/25
**Holstein** 26/27
**Horse shows** 38/39
**Hungary** 16/17
**Hydaspes, Battle of** 44/45
**Hyracotherium** 2/3

**Jockeys** 42/43

**Kladruber** 24/24
**Knabstrup** 24/25
**Knights in armor** 8/9

**Lipizzaner** 24/25
**Longbow** 8/9
**Lungeing** 32/33

**Mail coaches** 14/15, 16/17
**Mammals, early** 2/3
**Manipuri ponies** 40/41
**Morzillo** 12/13

**Nomad tribes** 6/7

**Olympics** 38/39
**Orlov Trotters** 26/27

**Pack horses** 28/29
**Palestine** 10/11
**Parthians** 10/11
**Pazyryk tombs** 6/7

**Pegasus** 44/45
**Percheron** 24/25
**Pit Ponies** 18/19
**Pliohippus** 2/3
**Pony Express** 14/15
**Postal Express** 14/15
**Postal systems** 14/15, 16/17
**Przevalski's horse** 6/7

**Quarter horse** 26/27
**Quaternary Epoch** 2/3

**Racing** 28/29, 42/43
**Romans** 6/7, 16/17
**Riding** 30/31, 32/33
**Rodeos** 32/33

**Saddles** 36/37
**Scythians** 6/7
**Shetland ponies** 18/19
**Shire horses** 20/21, 24/25
**Showjumping** 38/39
**Sloan, Ted** 42/43
**Stabling** 34/35
**Stagecoaches** 16/17
**Steeplechasing** 42/43
**Sybaris** 6/7

**Tournaments** 8/9
**Training methods** 32/33
**Trojan Horse** 44/45
**Trooping the Color** 20/21
**Trotting races** 26/27

**Unicorn** 44/45

**Warfare, horses in** 8/9, 10/11, 12/13
**Waterloo, Battle of** 12/13
**Wells Fargo** 16/17
**Welsh Mountain Pony** 24/25

**Photo-Credits**

4/5 French Government Tourist Office, 6/7 Michael Holford. 10/11 Michael Holford. 12/13 Mansell Collection. 18/19 Mansell Collection. 20/21 Whitbread & Co. Ltd., Alan Hutchison. 22/23 Peter Roberts, R.S.P.C.A. 24/25 Sally Anne Thompson, Peter Roberts. 26/27 Sally Anne Thompson, Popperfoto. 28/29 Sally Anne Thompson, W. W. Rouch. 32/33 J. Allan Cash Ltd. (Chipperfields Circus), Sampson Low. 34/35 Peter Roberts. 38/39 Colorsport, Peter Roberts. 40/41 Fotomas Index, Robert Harding Associates. 42/43 Sport & General Press. 44/45 Mary Evans Picture Library. Inside back cover: Fotomas Index.